Cambridge Primary

D1795275

Ready to Go Lessons for English

Step-by-step
lesson plans for
Cambridge Primary

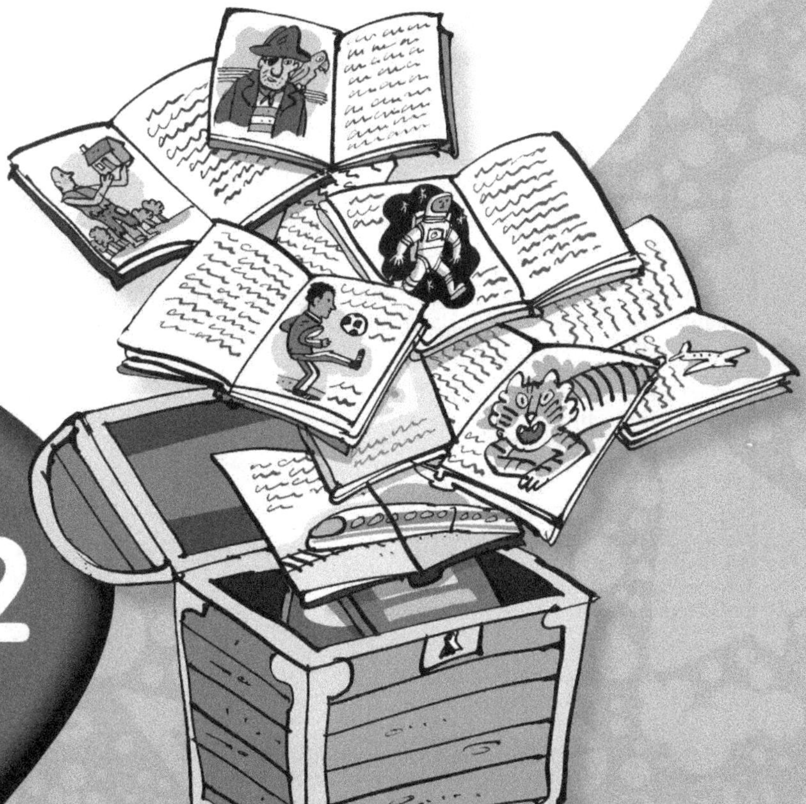

Stage 2

Kay Hiatt

Series editor: Emily Budinger

HODDER
EDUCATION
AN HACHETTE UK COMPANY

The Publishers would like to thank the following for permission to reproduce copyright material:

Acknowledgements
p9: Jeanne Willis, extract from *The Bog Baby* (Puffin Books, 2008), copyright Jeanne Willis, 2008, reprinted by permission of Penguin Books Ltd; **p.17:** Dianne Stewart, extract from *The Gift of the Sun: A Tale from South Africa* (Francis Lincoln Books, 2007), reprinted by permission of the publisher; **p.39:** Godfrey Hall, extract adapted from *Games (Traditions Around The World)* (Hodder Wayland, 1995), first published in the UK by Wayland, an imprint of Hachette Children's Books, 338 Euston Road, London NW1 3BH, reprinted by permission of the publisher; **p.45:** Ray Gibson, 'Making paper flowers', extract from *What Shall We Do Today?* (Usborne Books, 1995), copyright © 1995 Usborne Publishing Ltd, reprinted by permission of the publisher; **p.49:** 'Sweet and Spicy Popcorn' recipe, inspired by http://allrecipes.com/recipe/sweet-and-spicy-popcorn; **p.51:** Tony Bradman, 'The Sandwich' from *Twinkle Twinkle Chocolate Bar*, edited by John Foster (Oxford University Press, 2009), reprinted by permission of The Agency (London) Ltd. on behalf of Tony Bradman; **p.56:** Mike Jubb, 'The playtime puddle rhyme' from *More First Verses*, edited by John Foster (Oxford University Press, 1999), reprinted by permission of Mike Jubb: www.teachkidspoetry.co.uk; **p.57:** John Foster, 'You can't catch me' from *More First Verses*, edited by John Foster (Oxford University Press, 1999), reprinted by permission of the author; **p.59:** Gareth Owen, 'Jam on Toast' from *Gathering in the Days* (Collins Educational, 2011), reprinted by permission of Rogers, Coleridge & White Literary Agency, 20 Powis Mews, London W11 1JN, on behalf of Gareth Owen; Julia Donaldson, 'One Tongue' from *Crazy Mayonnaisy Mum* (Macmillan Children's Books, 2005), reprinted by permission of Macmillan Children's Books, London, UK; Mike Jubb, from 'Beans with everything' from *More First Verses*, edited by John Foster (Oxford University Press, 1999), reprinted by permission of Mike Jubb: www.teachkidspoetry.co.uk; **p.61:** Judith Nicholls, 'Bedtime, please!', © Judith Nicholls 1990, reprinted by permission of the author; Eleanor Farjeon, 'Bedtime' from *Blackbird Has Spoken: Selected Poems for Children* (Macmillan Children's Books, 1999), reprinted by permission of David Higham; **p.63:** Dorothy Aldis, 'The picnic'; Kenn Nesbitt, 'Our family picnic' from http://www.poetry4kids.com, reprinted by permission of the author; **p.65:** Stanley Cook, 'Tulips on the roundabout' from *Dark as a Midnight Dream: Poetry Collection 2*, compiled by Fiona Walters (Evans, 1998), reprinted by permission of The Poetry Business on behalf of the Estate of Stanley Cook; **p.117:** John Foster, 'Magic Horse' from *Twinkle Twinkle Chocolate Bar*, edited by John Foster (Oxford University Press, 2009), reprinted by permission of the author; **p.119:** Christina Rossetti, 'Is the moon tired'; Gareth Owen, 'Someone' from *Gathering in the Days* (Collins Educational, 2011), reprinted by permission of Rogers, Coleridge & White Literary Agency, 20 Powis Mews, London W11 1JN, on behalf of Gareth Owen; **p.121:** Julia Donaldson, 'Two Friends' from *Crazy Mayonnaisy Mum* (Macmillan Children's Books, 2005), copyright © Macmillan Children's Books 2005, reprinted by permission of Macmillan Children's Books, London, UK; **p.123:** Barry Buckingham, 'Three cheers' and Julie Holder, 'The Alien' from *Footprints on the Moon and Other Poems*, edited by Brian Moses (Hodder Wayland, 2010); **p.125:** Judith Nicholls, 'Ten things to eat beginning with G' and 'Eleven words to use instead of said ...' from *The Hamster Diaries and Other Kinds of Writing 1 (Oxford Primary English)*, compiled by Brian Moses (1992), reprinted by permission of Judith Nicholls; **p.127:** Michael Rosen, 'Colour' from www.michaelrosen.co.uk, and 'I know someone', both reprinted by permission of Peters Fraser & Dunlop (www.petersfraserdunlop.com) on behalf of Michael Rosen; **p.171:** Angela Wilkes, extracts adapted from *Question Time: Rainforest* (Kingfisher Books, 2002), copyright © Kingfisher, an imprint of Macmillan Publishers Ltd 2002, reprinted by permission of the publisher; **p.179:** Spike Milligan, 'On the Ning Nang Nong' from *Silly Verse for Kids* (Puffin Books, 1989), reprinted by permission of Spike Milligan Productions Ltd; 'Dr Bell' from *Michael Rosen's Book of Nonsense* (Hodder Children's Books, 1998); **p.181:** Michael Rosen, 'More, More, More' from *Michael Rosen's Book of Nonsense* (Hodder Children's Books, 1998); **p.183:** Michael Rosen, 'Night, night, Knight' from *Walking the Bridge of Your Nose: Wordplay, Poems and Rhymes* (Kingfisher Books, 1997), reprinted by permission of Peters Fraser & Dunlop (www.petersfraserdunlop.com) on behalf of Michael Rosen; Kitty Morrow, 'A big black bear' from 1st International Collection of Tongue Twisters, www.uebersetzung.at/twister/en.htm © 1996–2012 by Mr Twister; **p.185:** Michael Rosen, 'Yesterday' from *Michael Rosen's Book of Nonsense* (Hodder Children's Books, 1998); Michael Rosen, 'One bright September morning in the middle of July' from *Walking the Bridge of Your Nose: Wordplay, Poems and Rhymes* (Kingfisher Books, 1997), reprinted by permission of Peters Fraser & Dunlop (www.petersfraserdunlop.com) on behalf of Michael Rosen; **p.187:** Charles Causley, '"Quack!" Said the Billy-goat' from *I Had a Little Cat – Collected Poems for Children* (Macmillan Children's Books, 2009), reprinted by permission of David Higham; **p.189:** Michael Rosen, 'Help, Help' from *Michael Rosen's Book of Nonsense* (Hodder Children's Books, 1998); **p.192:** Edward Lear, 'There was an old man of Dumbree' from *More Nonsense – Pictures, Rhymes, Botany, etc* (1872).

Every effort has been made to trace all copyright holders, but if any have been inadvertently overlooked the Publishers will be pleased to make the necessary arrangements at the first opportunity.

Although every effort has been made to ensure that website addresses are correct at time of going to press, Hodder Education cannot be held responsible for the content of any website mentioned in this book. It is sometimes possible to find a relocated web page by typing in the address of the home page for a website in the URL window of your browser. Websites included in this text have not been reviewed as part of the Cambridge endorsement process.

Hachette UK's policy is to use papers that are natural, renewable and recyclable products and made from wood grown in sustainable forests. The logging and manufacturing processes are expected to conform to the environmental regulations of the country of origin.

Orders: please contact Bookpoint Ltd, 130 Milton Park, Abingdon, Oxon OX14 4SB. Telephone: (44) 01235 827720. Fax: (44) 01235 400454. Lines are open 9.00–5.00, Monday to Saturday, with a 24-hour message answering service. Visit our website at www.hoddereducation.com.

© Kay Hiatt 2013
First published in 2013 by
Hodder Education,
An Hachette UK Company
Carmelite House, 50 Victoria Embankment
London EC4Y 0DZ

Impression number   6
Year   2018

Cover illustration by Peter Lubach
Illustrations by Planman Technologies
Typeset in ITC Stone Serif Medium 10/12.5 by Planman Technologies
Printed in Great Britain by CPI Group (UK) Ltd, Croydon, CR0 4YY

A catalogue record for this title is available from the British Library.

ISBN: 978 1444 177053

Contents

Introduction

About the series

Ready to Go Lessons is a series of photocopiable resource books providing creative teaching strategies for primary teachers. These books support the revised Cambridge Primary curriculum frameworks for English, Mathematics and Science at Stages 1–6 (ages 5–11). They have been written by experienced primary teachers to reflect the different teaching approaches recommended in the Cambridge Primary Teacher Guides. The books contain lesson plans and photocopiable support materials, with a wide range of activities and appropriate ideas for assessment and differentiation. As the books are intended for international schools we have taken care to ensure that they are culturally sensitive.

Cambridge Primary

The Cambridge Primary curriculum frameworks show schools how to develop the learners' knowledge, skills and understanding in English, Mathematics and Science. They provide a secure foundation in preparation for the Cambridge Secondary 1 (lower secondary) curriculum. The ideas in this book can also be easily incorporated into existing curriculum frameworks already in your school.

How to use this book

This book covers each of the units of the scheme of work for English at Stage 2. It can be worked through systematically, or used to support areas where you feel you need more ideas. It is not prescriptive – it gives ideas and suggestions for you to incorporate into your own planning and teaching as you see fit.

Each step-by-step lesson plan shows you the learning objectives you will cover, the resources you will need and how to deliver the lesson. The lesson plans offer recommendations for suitable texts in the 'Resources' section, however the plans and photocopiable pages have been designed to be as flexible as possible so that if you don't have the specific text the lesson plan and photocopiable page can usually easily be adapted to use an alternative. Each lesson includes a Starter activity, Main activities and a Plenary that draws the lesson to a close and recaps the learning objectives. Success criteria are provided in the form of questions to help you assess the learners' level of understanding. The 'Differentiation' section provides support for the less-able learners and extension ideas for the more able.

For each lesson plan there is at least one supporting photocopiable activity page. At the end of each unit there are also suggestions for assessment activities. Answers to activities can be found at www.hoddereducation.com/cambridgeextras.

Learning objectives

The Cambridge Primary English curriculum framework provides a set of learning objectives for each stage. At the start of each lesson you need to re-phrase the learning objectives into child-friendly language so that you can share them with the learners at the outset. It sometimes helps to express them as *We are learning to / about …* statements or an enquiry question. This really does help the learners to focus on the lesson's outcomes. For example: 'Use reading as a model for writing dialogue' (Stage 3) could be introduced to the learners at the start of the lesson as: *We are learning to write direct speech.* To avoid unnecessary repetition we have not included such statements at the start of each lesson plan but it is understood that the teacher would do this.

The speaking and listening objectives have been creatively threaded through the units in order to actively engage the learners with the text type, supporting the *Talk for Writing* approaches. Similarly the grammar and punctuation objectives and skills have been linked into the reading and writing activities in order to contextualise the learning more fully.

Objective coverage

The overview chart on pages 6–7 shows you how the learning objectives are covered in the lessons in this book. You will notice that although the schemes of work include objectives for phonics, spelling and handwriting these have generally not been included in the books. *Letters and Sounds* suggests that good practice would be to teach a separate phonics, spelling and handwriting lesson. For that reason these books focus mainly on the vocabulary, grammar and punctuation, reading, writing, speaking and listening objectives. The objectives not covered in this book are: 2R01, 2R03, 2W01, 2W02, 2Ws1, 2Ws2, 2Ws3 and 2Ws4.

Success criteria

These are the measures that the teacher and, eventually, the learner will be able to use to assess the outcome of the learning that has taken place in each lesson. They are included as a series of questions, which will help you as teacher to assess the learners' understanding of the skills and knowledge covered in the lesson.

Formative assessment

Formative assessment is on-going assessment that occurs in every lesson and informs the teacher and learners of the progress they are making, linked to the success criteria. The types of questions to ask that will support teachers in making formative assessments have been incorporated into each lesson in the 'Success criteria' sections.

One of the advantages of formative assessment is that any problems that arise during the lesson can be responded to immediately. Formative assessment influences the next steps in learning and may influence changes in planning and / or delivery for subsequent lessons.

Summative assessment

Summative assessment is essential at the end of each unit of work to assess exactly what the learners know, understand and can do. The assessment sections at the end of each chapter are designed to provide you with a variety of opportunities to check the learners' understanding of the unit. These activities can include specific questions for teachers to ask, activities for the learners to carry out (independently, in pairs or in groups) or written assessment.

The information gained from both the formative and summative assessment ideas can then be used to inform future planning in order to close any gaps in the learners' understanding as recommended by *Assessment for Learning* (AFL).

Appropriate use of IT

At the planning stage teachers need to consider how the use of IT in a lesson will enhance the learning process. Ensure that the IT resources you use support and promote the learners' understanding of the learning objectives. Activities included in this book have been designed to be carried out without the need for state-of-the-art IT facilities. Suggestions have also been included for schools with internet access and / or the use of interactive whiteboards. This is in order to cater for most teachers' needs.

In these lessons the author sometimes asks for the teacher to display an enlarged version of the photocopiable page at the front of the class. We have not specified whether this should be using an overhead projector, interactive whiteboard or flipchart, as schools will have different resources available to them.

We hope that using these resources will give you confidence and creative ideas in delivering the Cambridge Primary English curriculum framework.

Emily Budinger, Series Editor

Overview chart

The Bog Baby

Learning objectives

- Identify and describe story settings and characters, recognising that they may be from different times and places. (2Ri2)
- Discuss the meaning of unfamiliar words encountered in reading. (2R10)
- Write using a variety of sentence types. (2Wp6)

Resources

Photocopiable page 9; *The Bog Baby* by Jeanne Willis (Puffin); pictures of local ponds; pictures of newts and frogs; internet access.

Starter

- Read *The Bog Baby* or watch it being read on the internet (for example at www.youtube.com/watch?v=mIdwsUEXscQ). Read the story a second time, pausing to ensure that the learners understand the theme of the story: that sometimes if you love something or someone, you have to let them go.
- Explain the meaning of some words the learners may not understand, showing images where possible, such as:
  - bog: a very wet, muddy area
  - newt: a small amphibian that looks like a small lizard, with a large tail
  - dell: a small valley in a wood
  - bluebells: blue, bell-shaped flowers on a stalk, which grow in great clusters in woods in Britain, Spain, France, Italy and North Africa.

Main activities

- Ask: *What did you enjoy about this story?* Take a few opinions from the learners.
- Write further questions about the story on the board and ask the learners to discuss the answers together in pairs, for example:
  - *Who are the characters?*
  - *Where does the story take place?*
  - *Could this story happen locally? (Are there wooded areas with ponds?)*

- Display an enlarged version of photocopiable page 9. Together with the learners, read the description of the Bog Baby and what he liked doing.
- Give each learner photocopiable page 9 to complete. Suggest that their sentences could be about:
  - what the Bog Baby looks like
  - what he can do
  - what he likes doing best.

Plenary

- Hand out a selection of statements about the Bog Baby to small groups of learners, for example:
  - He lives in cool and damp places.
  - He is more like a frog than a fish.
  - He likes eating cake crumbs.
- Ask the groups to discuss whether their statements are true or false. After the discussion, ask a learner from each group to read out one statement, saying whether it is true or false and giving evidence from the text.

Success criteria

Ask the learners:

- Describe the setting for this story.
- Who are the characters that appear in this story?
- What is a dell and what is a newt?
- Tell me a sentence about the Bog Baby that has two facts with the word *and* joining these facts.

Ideas for differentiation

Support: Provide these learners with some partially written sentences about the Bog Baby that they can finish, for example: 'He was the size of a ...', 'He was round and ...'

Extension: Ask these learners to write a few sentences in which the Bog Baby says why he loves the wood.

Name: _____

The Bog Baby

1.   Read the description of the Bog Baby below.

'He was the size of a frog, only round and blue.

He had boggly eyes and a spiky tail

and I do remember he had ears like a mouse.

He came swinging through the flower stalks

and jumped into the water.

He floated up and down on his

back and sucked his toes.'

From **The Bog Baby** by Jeanne Willis

2.   Draw a picture of a bog baby in the box below and label parts of his body.

The Bog Baby

3.   Write three sentences about the Bog Baby.

_____

_____

_____

Writing in role

Learning objectives

- Talk about what happens at the beginning, in the middle or at the end of a story. (2Rw2)
- Extend experiences and ideas through role-play. (2SL9)
- Begin to re-read own writing aloud to check for sense and accuracy. (2W03)

Resources

Photocopiable page 11.

Starter

- Organise the learners into small groups and give each group one of the following scenes from *The Bog Baby* by Jeanne Willis (Puffin) to prepare as a freeze-frame. Tell them to allocate parts (including trees and sound effects, depending on the group size) and to discuss how they will capture the scene as a freeze-frame. (Allow the sisters to become brothers if necessary.) Ask the learners to discuss whether their scene is from the beginning, middle or end of the story.
  - Scene 1: The two sisters are sitting thinking about what they might do today.
  - Scene 2: The sisters are walking through the wood then arriving at the pond.
  - Scene 3: The two sisters are going into the shed; one is carrying the Bog Baby in a jam jar.
  - Scene 4: The two sisters show the Bog Baby to two friends.
  - Scene 5: In the shed, Mum is standing looking at the two sisters, who are sitting looking at her.
  - Scene 6: In groups of three, Mum is looking on while the sisters put the Bog Baby back in the pond.
- Ask the groups to get in their starting positions and then to 'Freeze!' when you say so.

Main activities

- Now ask the learners to improvise actions and conversations for their scenes, for example:
  - Scene 1: Talking about what they might do today.

- Scene 2: Walking through the wood, fishing, finding the Bog Baby and talking about him.
- Scene 3: Making a home for him.
- Scene 4: Meeting with friends and showing them the Bog Baby.
- Scene 5: Talking about why they must take him back.
- Scene 6: Putting the Bog Baby back into the pond.
- Ask the groups to perform their scenes in turn.
- Hand out photocopiable page 11 for the learners to complete individually.
- When they have finished writing, ask them to re-read their writing and check for meaning and accuracy.

Plenary

- Ask different learners to read out their thought bubbles from photocopiable page 11 without saying which character's thoughts they are.
- Ask the other learners to work out who is saying what and to give their views on what was written.

Success criteria

Ask the learners:

- Which events happened at the beginning of the story?
- How did this story end?
- How did role-play help you get inside the story?
- Did you feel like one of the characters?
- Why is it important to re-read your own writing?

Ideas for differentiation

Support: Ask these learners to write one thing the girls did that was good, and one thing the girls did that was bad.

Extension: Ask these learners to read the last page of the book, 'Notes about your Bog Baby', and to complete the answers to share with the rest of the class.

Name: _____

I remember the Bog Baby

What do you think each character would remember about the day they found a Bog Baby in the woods? Write their thoughts below.

Mum: I remember ...

Chrissy: I remember ...

Chrissy's
sister: I remember ...

Bog Baby: I remember ...

Talking and thinking about the story

Learning objectives

- Use phonics as the main method of tackling unfamiliar words. (2R02)
- Extend the range of common words recognised on sight. (2R04)
- Begin to develop likes and dislikes in reading and listening to stories drawing on background information and vocabulary provided. (2R05)

Resources

Photocopiable page 13; book evaluation pages.

Starter

- Display an enlarged version of photocopiable page 13, covering up all the questions apart from the first.
- Give the learners time to read the question silently.
- Ask them to read the question aloud.
- Point to each word in turn, encouraging the learners to use phonics as the main method of tackling any unknown words.
- Do not discuss possible answers at this stage.
- Reveal the other questions in turn, carrying out the same reading process for each one.
- Highlight all the sight words the learners know and others that are new, reading these without using phonic skills. Make a class chart and add a selection of new words in a different colour.

Main activities

- Cut the questions from photocopiable page 13 into individual sentence strips and put them in a hat.
- Invite different learners to take a question out of the hat, read it aloud and then stick it to the board.
- Ask the learners to think about each question in turn, then listen as you ask selected learners to give their thoughts and views.
- Ask the learners to work in pairs to prepare their own answers to two or three of the questions, using a creative way to capture their answer, for example: film an improvised scene that explains

their answer, photograph a freeze-frame, draw a poster (such as a warning poster including the words 'Keep out – dangerous pond'), draw a picture (for example of the magical pond), record an interview with a character in the hot seat, write a letter, and so on.

- Hand out book evaluation pages (with headings such as 'Name of book', 'What is the book about?', 'Did you enjoy the book? Why or why not?', 'Would you recommend the book to a friend?'). Ask the learners to record their thoughts about *The Bog Baby* by Jeanne Willis (Puffin).

Plenary

- Ask pairs of learners to display their answers to the questions from photocopiable page 13. Organise time to watch and listen to any answers that have been recorded using IT.
- Discuss the different answers and the different ways they were captured. Make time for the learners to comment on each others' efforts.
- Discuss further ideas the learners have about any answers to the questions, or further ideas they've had about capturing their answers.
- Ask different learners to talk about their evaluation pages and their overall feelings about *The Bog Baby*. Did everyone think they would recommend it to a friend?

Success criteria

Ask the learners:

- How can you use sounds to help you read a word?
- Why do you need to read questions carefully?
- Why should you take time to think carefully about your answers?
- Have you ever read a book because a friend said it was good?

Ideas for differentiation

Support: Working on the questions in mixed-ability groups will help these learners to become more confident in answering questions.

Extension: Challenge these learners to come up with very original ways of recording their answers.

The Bog Baby

1. Who would have told the girls not to go into the wood by themselves?

2. Why is a visit to the wood 'not allowed'?

3. What is special about the magic pond?

4. Why do the girls like the Bog Baby so much?

5. Why do the girls decide to take the Bog Baby home?

6. Why don't the girls tell Mum about the Bog Baby?

7. How do the girls make a new home for the Bog Baby?

8. How do the girls know that the Bog Baby is sick?

9. How does Mum explain to the girls why they have to take the Bog Baby back to the pond?

10. Why do the girls take the Bog Baby back to the wood?

11. What is the lovely surprise at the end?

12. Could children learn anything from this story?

The Gift of the Sun

Learning objectives

- Discuss the meaning of unfamiliar words encountered in reading. (2R10)
- Identify and describe story settings and characters, recognising that they may be from different times and places. (2Ri2)
- Predict story endings. (2Ri1)

Resources

The Gift of the Sun by Dianne Stewart and Jude Daly (Frances Lincoln); map of the world or a globe; some sunflower seeds; photocopiable page 15.

Starter

- Show the learners the cover of *The Gift of the Sun* and ask them to read the title and other text on the cover.
- Locate South Africa on a map of the world – is their school near this country?
- Ask the learners what the farmer is doing in the picture on the cover.
- Do the learners know the name of the flowers on the cover? Have they noticed that the hens and chicks seem to like the seeds?
- Hand out sunflower seeds for the learners to feel and talk about (ensuring first that no one is allergic to nuts).

Main activities

- Explain the meaning of any unfamiliar words, for example 'bask', 'nuisance', 'dew', 'fleece', 'shear', 'unfurled'.
- Read the story up to the point where Dora is very pleased because the hens are laying more eggs.
- Organise the learners into four groups and hand out photocopiable page 15 to each group.
- In their groups, ask the learners to read the three events outlined on the photocopiable page and to discuss what they think happens next, supporting their views. Move around the groups, listening to their opinions.

- Ask the learners individually to choose an event and then finish writing the story.
- Now finish reading the book and compare their choice of ending with the actual ending.

Plenary

- Using the words from the start of the 'Main activities' section, ask the learners to give you the word when you give its definition, for example: *Can you think of another word for 'naughty'?* (Nuisance.) *Which word means 'to lie in the sun'?* (Bask.)
- Write the following statements on the board then ask the learners to discuss in small groups which one is most likely and how it might finish: 'I think Dora and Thulani will be happy now because …' and 'I think Dora and Thulani will not be happy now because …'

Success criteria

Ask the learners:

- Where is the setting for this story?
- Are the weather and land different from where you live?
- Do Dora and Thulani work well as a team on the farm?
- Explain what the words 'bask', 'dew' and 'fleece' mean.
- Which word tells you that the sheep have their fleeces cut off?
- Did you predict the right ending for the book?

Ideas for differentiation

Support: Arrange for an adult to join these learners to read out and discuss the possible endings with them.

Extension: When these learners have finished photocopiable page 15, ask them to write a letter to Thulani warning him not to become lazy again.

Name: _____

What happened next?

1. What do you think will happen next in **The Gift of the Sun**?
    Choose from these three suggestions:

Event 1

Thulani is too lazy to shut the door of the shed where the sunflower seeds are stored. The rats get in and eat them all. The next day Dora …

Event 2

Thulani is too lazy to go to the market to sell the eggs, and they all go bad! The next day Dora …

Event 3

Thulani and Dora are very tired and do not hear the noise when the fox gets in and eats lots of chickens. The remaining chickens are so upset they stop laying eggs …

---

2. Write your prediction of what will happen next and how the story ends. Use one of the events above and then continue it with your own ideas to end the story.

_____

_____

_____

_____

Thulani and Dora

Learning objectives

● Make simple inferences from the words on the page, e.g. about feelings. (2Ri3)

● Begin to read with fluency and expression, taking some notice of punctuation, including speech marks. (2R07)

● Begin to be aware of ways in which speakers vary talk, e.g. the use of more formal vocabulary and tone of voice. (2SL10)

Resources

The Gift of the Sun by Dianne Stewart and Jude Daly (Frances Lincoln); happy and sad faces on sticks; photocopiable page 17.

Starter

• Tell the learners that they are going to be book detectives. Explain that the author has hidden clues inside the sentences that show how Thulani and Dora are feeling. The clues may be in dialogue or the narrated parts of the book (ensure the learners know the difference).

• Give out the happy and sad faces on sticks.

• Write the first sentence from photocopiable page 17 on the board: "I am tired of all this milking."

• Ask the learners to read this silently.

• Now ask them which words tell us that Thulani does not like milking the cow. ('tired'; 'all this milking'.)

• Underline the words and read the sentence with fluency and expression to show his feelings: 'I am <u>tired</u> of <u>all</u> this <u>milking</u>.'

• Explain to the learners that reading with expression gives you clues to how characters are feeling.

• Ask the class which picture card should be used to show how Thulani is feeling at the moment. (The sad face.)

Main activities

• Hand out photocopiable page 17 to the learners in pairs and ask them to work together to complete the tasks.

• Call the class back together again and ask different pairs of the learners to say which words they have underlined.

• Ask different learners to read these sentences expressively, to show the characters' feelings.

• Ask the other learners to select the happy or sad face and hold it up.

Plenary

• Ask the learners to listen to you reading the page beginning 'Early one morning …' **without** any expression in your voice, then again **with** expression in your voice.

• Ask them which reading gave them more clues to the characters' feelings – the first or the second one, and to say why.

• Ask the learners in pairs to discuss what they learnt about Thulani and Dora's feelings.

Success criteria

Ask the learners:

● How do you know that characters are speaking in books?

● How can the author of a book show you how characters feel?

● Why is it good to read with expression in your voice?

Ideas for differentiation

Support: Ask an adult helper to read the sentences with expression to these learners to help them locate the words of interest. Ask them to hold up the smiling or unsmiling face to show whether the character is happy or sad.

Extension: Ask these learners to role-play a conversation that Dora might have with a friend, telling the friend all about what Thulani is doing at the farm.

Name: _____

Reading detectives

1. Read the sentences below. Look for the clues that tell you how the characters are feeling. Underline the words that are the clues. The first one has been done for you.

Thulani said, "I am <u>tired</u> of <u>all this milking</u>."

"Oh Thulani!" sighed Dora, his wife. "You've sold the cow and now we'll have no milk!"

"Wake up, Thulani!" shouted Dora. "That nuisance goat has eaten all our seed!"

Thulani felt sad.

Dora said, "Thulani, we need seed, not geese."

"Thulani," said Dora excitedly, "these hens are laying more than ever before."

At last Thulani had done something right!

From **The Gift of the Sun** by Dianne Stewart and Jude Daly

2. Now practise reading the lines above with expression to show how the characters are feeling.

Learning about sentences

Learning objectives

- Use mainly simple and compound sentences, with *and / but* to connect ideas. *Because* may begin to be used in a complex sentence. (2Wp3)
- Articulate clearly so that others can hear. (2SL3)
- Demonstrate 'attentive listening' and engage with another speaker. (2SL8)

Resources

Photocopiable page 19; pictures of food.

Starter

- Tell the learners that you are going to play a game to practise using 'and', 'but' and 'because' in sentences.
- Ask the learners to give you names of food they like and dislike, and write these on the board.
- Model combining phrases with the connective 'and', 'but' or 'because' in turn, for example: 'I like spaghetti **and** I like beans'; 'I like cheese **but** I don't like eggs'; 'I like apples **because** they're sweet'.
- Leaving the food words displayed, sit the learners in a circle and challenge them to say a sentence about food using one of the connectives, going around the circle until everyone has had a turn. Explain that they may not use the connective that the learner before them used.
- Ask the learners to turn to a partner and discuss the difference between these two sentences: 'I like apples **and** pears' and 'I like apples **because** they're sweet'. (The first sentence gives two facts; the second one gives a fact and a reason.)

Main activities

- Write the following sentence on the board: 'Thulani loved basking in the sun … did not like milking the cow'. Ask: *Which connective should go in the space?*
- Hand out photocopiable page 19 and ask the learners to complete the task with a partner, listening to each other's point of view.

- Select different learners to read out their sentences clearly for all to hear. When two different connectives work in the same sentence, discuss the different meanings.

Plenary

- Divide the learners into three teams and display a number of words around a topic, for example: 'reading books', 'watching television', 'listening to music', 'cycling', 'swimming', 'going to the seaside'.
- Call out 'and', 'but' or 'because' and challenge the teams to use the words to make up a sentence about the topic with that connective in it in 10 seconds. Give the teams a point every time they create a suitable sentence in the time.

Success criteria

Ask the learners:

- Give me a sentence that uses the word 'but'.
- Which connectives join two facts?
- Why is it important to speak clearly so that others can hear?
- How would someone know that you are listening really carefully to what they are saying?
- Why is it important to listen to someone carefully before you reply to them?

Ideas for differentiation

Support: Ask these learners to play the connectives game using pictures of food and orally joining sentences with 'and', 'but' or 'because'.

Extension: Ask these learners to write three sentences each about *The Gift of the Sun* using the word 'because'.

Name: _____

Missing connectives

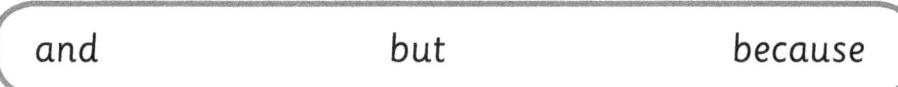

Choose the connective you think is missing from each sentence:

| and | but | because |

1. Thulani decided to sell the cow _____ buy a goat.

2. He left early in the morning _____ it was cool.

3. He came home with a goat _____ Dora was not pleased.

4. The goat went into the house _____ ate all their corn.

5. Thulani sold the goat _____ bought a sheep.

6. Dora liked the sheep _____ they could sell the fleece.

7. Thulani sold the sheep _____ the fleece and bought three geese.

8. Dora was cross _____ geese ate too much food.

9. Thulani sold the geese _____ bought some seed.

10. The plants grew _____ they were sunflowers.

Story writing

Learning objectives

- Use the structures of familiar poems and stories in developing own writing. (2W05)
- Begin to use dialogue in stories. (2Wa4)
- Build and use collections of interesting and significant words. (2Wa3)

Resources

Photocopiable pages 19 and 21; multiple copies of photocopiable page 19 cut up into individual sentences.

Starter

- Display an enlarged version of photocopiable page 19 with all the connectives in place. Read these through with the learners.
- Hand out the cut-up versions to the learners in small groups and ask them to divide up these events into three sections: Beginning, Middle and End. (Beginning: 1–3; Middle: 3–8; End: 9–10.)

Main activities

- Read the first four sentences together and then ask the learners to think of something one of the characters might say at this point, for example: "I wish you had never bought that goat!" yelled Dora.
- Write it on the board, recapping on the rules of punctuating dialogue and highlighting the speech marks as you do so.
- Now read the words with expression, and then ask the learners to copy you, reminding them to articulate clearly so others can hear.
- Ask them why 'yelled' is a better word than 'said'.
- Now ask the learners to read sentences 6–8 with a partner and come up with some speech for this section, for example: '"Buying that sheep was a **big** mistake. Now I can **never** bask in the sun again," sobbed Thulani.' Encourage them to write their speech down and punctuate it correctly.

- Now that they are very familiar with this story, explain that they are going to write their own version. Provide each learner with the planning frame on photocopiable page 21 to plan their story first. Tell them to write a short exchange of dialogue between the two characters for each section.

Plenary

- Display a range of verbs for speech, such as 'shouted', 'laughed', 'yelled', 'whispered', 'roared', 'giggled'. Ask the learners to help you divide them into 'happy verbs' and 'unhappy verbs'. Some verbs might be found in both boxes, for example 'cried'.
- Read out the following bits of speech and ask the learners to suggest an appropriate verb, giving a reason for their choice, for example:
  - "STOP!" ... Mum outside the school gate.
  - "Look at us doing cartwheels!" ... the three girls.
  - "I am the biggest, strongest giant in the whole world!" ... the giant.

Success criteria

Ask the learners:

- What is the first part of the story called?
- How does this story (*The Gift of the Sun* by Dianne Stewart and Jude Daly [Frances Lincoln]) end?
- When writing, say why you need capital letters and full stops.
- What must you remember about punctuating dialogue?

Ideas for differentiation

Support: Ask these learners to draw a picture for each section of the story and give each character a speech bubble.

Extension: Challenge these learners to create longer dialogue between the two characters for each section of the story.

Name: _____

Planning a story

Use this frame to plan your story.

Beginning

_____
_____
_____
_____
_____
_____

Middle

_____
_____
_____
_____
_____
_____

Ending

_____
_____
_____
_____
_____

Amazing Grace

Learning objectives

- Talk about what happens at the beginning, in the middle or at the end of a story. (2Rw2)
- Read and respond to question words, e.g. *what, where, when, who, why.* (2Rx1)
- Demonstrate 'attentive listening' and engage with another speaker. (2SL8)

Resources

Amazing Grace by Mary Hoffman and Caroline Binch (Frances Lincoln); photocopiable page 23; dressing-up clothes for favourite characters from stories, films, television shows.

Starter

- Tell the learners that their new book is about a girl called Grace who loves pretending to be characters from books, television and films.
- Ask the learners if they ever pretend to be different people when they are playing with friends or at home. Do they walk, talk and act like their favourite characters?
- Invite some of the learners to act out a character and see if the other learners can guess who they are.

Main activities

- Show the learners the cover of *Amazing Grace* and focus on the picture of Grace.
- Read the opening section of the book – up to the scene at home where she is role-playing being a doctor – and then ask the learners:
  - *Grace loves all kinds of stories. Where does she get her stories from?*
  - *Grace likes to act out stories. What are some of the parts she likes to play?*
  - *Why do you think she likes these parts?*
  - *Do the illustrations help you to see that she loves acting?*
  - *Grace uses her imagination to pretend she is different people. What does the word 'imagination' mean?* (Making up and creating new ideas.)

- Tell the learners that they will now have the chance to use their imaginations. Give each learner photocopiable page 23 and, in pairs, give them time to talk about and discuss the characters they see on the photocopiable page. Ask them to complete the page individually.

Plenary

- Ask the learners to create a series of freeze-frames based on the characters they have chosen. Encourage them to use dressing-up clothes and to 'strike a pose' like Grace does in the book.
- Then invite the other learners to ask questions like: *Who are you? Why do you want to act out this character?*

Success criteria

Ask the learners:

- How does the story (*Amazing Grace*) start?
- What have we learnt about Grace's family so far?
- Where does Grace learn about all these characters?
- Think of a question to ask Grace about her friends at school.
- Why is it important to talk and listen to your partner when discussing something?

Ideas for differentiation

Support: Ask these learners to look through a collection of fairy tales, find a character they would like to be and 'strike a pose'. Share these with the class during the Plenary session.

Extension: Ask these learners: *What did her Nana and her Ma think of Grace's acting? How do you know?*

Name: _____

Famous characters

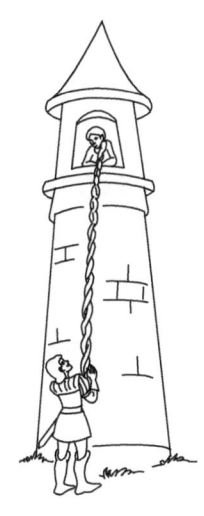

1. Choose any character you like from the table below.

2. Imagine what you could do if you were that character!

3. If you cannot find the name of your favourite character, write it in the empty box.

Rapunzel	Sleeping Beauty	Anansi	Peter Pan
Tinkerbell	Jack	Shrek	Harry Potter
Cinderella	Puss in Boots	Scooby Doo	Darth Vader
Belle	Hansel	Captain Hook	Superman
Dr Who	Power Ranger	The Little Mermaid	

4. Complete these sentences:

a) I would like to be _____.

b) If I was her / him I would _____

_____

_____

Talking about Grace

Learning objectives

- Make simple inferences from the words on the page, e.g. about feelings. (2Ri3)
- Talk about what happens at the beginning, in the middle or at the end of a story. (2Rw2)
- Extend experiences and ideas through role-play. (2SL9)

Resources

Amazing Grace by Mary Hoffman and Caroline Binch (Frances Lincoln); photocopiable page 25; an illustrated version of *Peter Pan* by J.M. Barrie (an abridged or Disney version is fine); a range of true and false statements about the characters from *Amazing Grace* (e.g. 'Raj didn't know that girls can play boys' parts', 'Ma was always very calm and never got angry'); a hat; two hoops.

Starter

- Re-read the double-page spread in *Amazing Grace* that begins 'One day at school ...'
- Ask the learners to look closely at the illustrations to work out how many of the children wanted to be Peter Pan (eight out of nine).
- Talk about the story of *Peter Pan*, showing pictures from the copy you have.
- Ask the learners if they can understand why Grace and most of the others wanted to play the part of Peter Pan so much.

Main activities

- Divide the learners into groups of three and ask each group to sort themselves into the roles of Raj, Natalie and Grace.
- Ask them to practise acting out the conversations between the children in the book, using expression to capture the emotions.
- Ask the learners to say how they felt saying these spiteful words or being Grace hearing them.
- Re-read the pages from 'When Grace got home' to 'I can even be Peter Pan'.

- Ask all the learners to practise saying what her Nana told Grace: 'You can be anything you want, Grace, if you put your mind to it.'
- Organise the learners into mixed-ability pairs and give each pair photocopiable page 25. Ask them to discuss and answer these questions together.
- Ask the learners to write two thought bubbles for Grace, showing her feelings about playing Peter Pan: the first capturing her thoughts after her conversation with Raj and Natalie; the second after her visit to the ballet with her Nana.
- Share the learners' thought bubbles.
- Now read the ending of the book.

Plenary

- Place the true and false statements in a hat and place the two hoops on the ground. Label the hoops TRUE and FALSE. Ask the learners to take out a statement, read it aloud and decide where to place it. The other learners can agree or disagree before the next statement is taken from the box.

Success criteria

Ask the learners:

- Which words did Raj say that showed he didn't want Grace to have the part?
- Which words did Nana say that made Grace feel she could play the part?
- How did the story end?
- What have you learnt from this story?

Ideas for differentiation

Support: Provide a template for the thought bubbles for these learners to complete.

Extension: Ask these learners to complete a third bubble that will be the teacher's views of whether Grace might be chosen as Peter Pan.

Questions about Amazing Grace

With a partner, answer the following questions:

1. Grace really wants to play Peter Pan. Why do Raj and Natalie

    say she can't play the part? _____

    _____

2. Do you think they are being fair to Grace by saying this? _____

    _____

3. Grace still keeps her hand up. Why doesn't she put it down again?

    _____

4. Ma tells Grace that Peter Pan is always played by a girl in pantomime.

    How does Grace feel when Ma tells her this? _____

    _____

5. Why do you think Ma starts to get angry when Grace tells her

    what Natalie said? _____

    _____

6. What does Nana say to make things better? _____

    _____

7. Nana takes Grace to the theatre. Why do you think she wanted

    to show Grace the ballet dancer? _____

    _____

8. Grace dances round the room like the ballet dancer. What has

    she learnt about herself by going to the ballet? _____

    _____

Grammar revision and practice

Learning objectives

- Write in clear sentences using capital letters, full stops and question marks. (2Wp1)
- Use past and present tenses accurately (if not always consistently). (2Wp4)
- Begin to use dialogue in stories. (2Wa4)

Resources

Photocopiable page 27.

Starter

- Read out the short dictation below to make sure that the learners can use full stops and capital letters correctly. Read one sentence at a time, with a long pause after every sentence, and ask the learners to write down what you have said:
  - *Grace lived with her Ma and Nana. They had a cat called Paw-Paws. Her Nana told her lots of stories.*
- Move around the class looking at what the learners are writing.
- Write examples of (anonymous) errors on the board and ask the learners to explain what is wrong and how to correct it.

Main activities

- Tell the learners that stories are usually written in the past tense – someone is telling you a story that has already happened.
- Create a series of statements in the present tense based on the story of *Amazing Grace* by Mary Hoffman and Caroline Binch (Frances Lincoln), or another book you are reading, for example:
  - Grace loves stories.
  - Grace acts them out.
  - Grace goes into battle as Joan of Arc.
  - Grace weaves a wicked web as Anansi.
- Read out your present-tense statements one at a time and ask the learners as a class to say them back to you in the past tense.
- Continue to make up statements as you go through the book.

- Remind the learners of the work they have done on speech marks (see page 20). Give each learner photocopiable page 27 to complete.
- When these have been completed, run through the sentences with the whole class, showing correct and incorrect versions.

Plenary

- Ask the learners to work in pairs to re-play the present-tense / past-tense game, with one learner making up (or remembering) present-tense statements for their partner to change into the past tense. Ask them to swap roles after a few minutes.
- As a whole class, ask different learners to find a piece of dialogue in a book and to read it out. Write the dialogue on the board and ask the other learners to tell you where to place the speech marks correctly.

Success criteria

Ask the learners:

- Why do sentences start with a capital letter?
- Why do sentences need to finish with a full stop or a question mark?
- Which tense are stories usually written in?
- Why is that tense (the past) used?
- Why are speech marks used?

Ideas for differentiation

Support: Give these learners a toy mobile phone and ask them to 'talk' to each other in the present tense: *Hello. I'm Alma. My best friend is Jasmina.*

Extension: Ask these learners to continue writing this poem all in (the past) tense:
When I was one I played my drum.
When I was two I tied my shoe.

Name: _____

Speech marks

The speech marks are missing in the dialogue below between Nana and her best friend, Susan. Write out each sentence correctly on the lines below. The first one has been done for you.

1. My Grace loves stories you know, said Nana.

    <u>"My Grace loves stories you know," said Nana.</u>

2. Which are her favourites? asked Susan.

    _____

3. She loves the Anansi stories best of all, said Nana.

    _____

4. Which one does she like the best? asked Susan.

    _____

5. She loves the one about Anansi and the Snake, said Nana.

    _____

    _____

6. Why does she love it so much? asked Susan.

    _____

7. Because Tiger asks Anansi to catch the biggest snake in the jungle and he does! said Nana.

    _____

    _____

Writing the story

Learning objectives

- Develop stories with a setting, characters and a sequence of events. (2Wa1)
- Structure a story with a beginning, middle and end. (2Wt1)
- Begin to re-read own writing aloud to check for sense and accuracy. (2W03)

Resources

Photocopiable pages 21 and 29.

Starter

- Ask the learners some quick-fire questions to check their knowledge of the sequence of events in *Amazing Grace* by Mary Hoffman and Caroline Binch (Frances Lincoln). Say: *Grace was a girl who loved stories*, then ask:
  - *How had she heard lots of stories?*
  - *Who were some of the characters she acted out?*
  - *How do you know she was good at acting?*
  - *Which part did she want in the school play?*
  - *What made her upset at school?*
  - *How did her Ma and Nana help her feel good again?*
  - *Why was she given the part?*
  - *Why did she say she felt as if she could fly all the way home?*

Main activities

- Now explain to the learners that they are going to write the story in their own words.
- Provide the planning frame on photocopiable page 21 for the learners to jot down some words and ideas against each section.
- Give each learner the success criteria on photocopiable page 29 for them to refer to as they write.
- Remind them to:
  - write the story in the past tense
  - use capital letters and full stops for sentences
  - add some dialogue if they want to – with correct use of speech marks
  - write some sentences with the connectives 'and', 'but' and 'because'.

- Encourage them to re-read their story as they go along, checking it makes sense. Once they have finished they can check it again against the success criteria. They can then illustrate their story if they wish.
- When they have finished, allow the learners in groups time to read aloud what they have written.

Plenary

- Arrange a table-top display of the finished stories and give time for the learners to move around and read them. Ask the learners to place a sticky note that says something good about what they have seen on every story, for example: 'I liked your drawings.', 'Your story was good.', 'I liked your dialogue.'
- Invite the learners to choose a selection of stories and give more details as to why they liked them.

Success criteria

Ask the learners:

- What do you call the place where stories happen?
- Why are characters important in stories?
- Do stories need to have a beginning, a middle and an ending?
- Why is it important to check that your writing makes sense, and that your spelling and punctuation are correct?

Ideas for differentiation

Support: Ask these learners to draw a picture of the part of *Amazing Grace* they like best, and write some captions.

Extension: Ask these learners to write a letter to Grace in which they tell her about some of the stories they have read, which she might enjoy.

Name: _____

Success criteria for writing

Use this page to check you have written your best story.

Success criteria:	First check	Second check
I wrote my story in the past tense by using words like 'went', 'ran', 'smiled' and 'walked'.	☺ ☹	☺ ☹
I used full stops and capital letters in the right places.	☺ ☹	☺ ☹
I used dialogue and speech marks to show who was speaking.	☺ ☹	☺ ☹
I made my sentences interesting by using 'and', 'but' and 'because'.	☺ ☹	☺ ☹
I checked my story by reading as I went along.	☺ ☹	☺ ☹
I have included an illustration.	☺ ☹	☺ ☹

Unit assessment

- Explain where all these stories are set.
- Explain why one of these three main characters is interesting: Chrissy from *The Bog Baby*, Thulani from *The Gift of the Sun* or Grace from *Amazing Grace.*

- What is dialogue?
- Explain why writers put dialogue into a story.
- What is the correct way to punctuate dialogue?

Summative assessment activities

Observe the learners while they play these games. You will quickly be able to identify those who may need additional support.

Story elements quiz

This game helps the learners to revisit the characterisation, settings and story openings of the stories in this unit.

You will need:

The three books for this unit placed on display (*The Bog Baby* by Jeanny Willis [Puffin], *The Gift of the Sun* by Dianne Stewart and Jude Daly and *Amazing Grace* by Mary Hoffman and Caroline Binch [both Frances Lincoln]); nine questions for each book – three about the characters, three about the setting and three about the opening (for example: 'Which character wants to take her friend to a magic pool?', 'Which story takes place on a farm in South Africa?', 'Which story starts by describing what the character loves doing?').

What to do

- Write the questions on separate pieces of paper and place them in a pile.
- Divide the learners into three equal teams and ask the teams to number themselves within their groups.
- Take a question from the pile and ask it to Team A, Player 1. If they get it right give them a point; if they get it wrong pass it over to Team B, Player 1. When the question has been successfully answered, ask the second question to Team B, Player 1.
- Carry on asking the learners questions in turn and keeping score. Celebrate the winning team.

Story openings

This activity assesses if the learners can write a story opening in the style of *The Gift of the Sun* and *Amazing Grace.*

You will need:

The Gift of the Sun by Dianne Stewart and Jude Daly and *Amazing Grace* by Mary Hoffman and Caroline Binch (both Frances Lincoln).

What to do

- Read the opening lines of *The Gift of the Sun* and *Amazing Grace.*
- Model how to use the same structure to write the opening of a new story using characters the learners are familiar with, for example: 'Cinderella was a girl who loved dancing.' or 'Batman was a man who loved helping people in trouble.'
- Ask the learners to take turns to say an opening line like this using a character of their choice and the same sentence structure.

Re-read *The Bog Baby* by Jeanne Willis (Puffin) with the learners. Give each learner photocopiable page 31 to complete. This will help to assess their knowledge and understanding of the story.

Name: _____

The Bog Baby quiz

1. Answer these questions about **The Bog Baby** by Jeanne Willis.

    a) What was special about the magic pond?

    _____

    b) Why did the girls decide to take the Bog Baby home?

    _____

    c) Why didn't they tell their mum about the Bog Baby?

    _____

    d) How did they make a new home for the Bog Baby?

    _____

    e) How did they know that the Bog Baby was sick?

    _____

    f) Why did they take him back to the wood?

    _____

2. Now choose a character you know well from a book, television series or film. Draw a picture of them below. Add labels to show special things about them.

Unit 1B: Instructions

Playground games

Starter

- Ask the learners what they remember about the way instructions are written. (A heading, a list of ingredients / resources, a 'What to do' section, and so on.)
- Play a game of 'Follow my leader' outside, taking the first turn as leader yourself to demonstrate the game (see instructions below).

Main activities

- As a piece of shared writing, write a set of instructions for playing 'Follow my leader' on the board, for example:

Follow my leader

1. Choose a leader.
2. Form a line behind the leader.
3. Follow the leader around the playground, copying what they do (hopping, crawling, side-stepping, and so on).
4. After a few minutes, choose a new leader.

- Ask the learners to read these instructions together and tell you:
  - why the instructions need a title
  - why bossy words are important in instructions
  - why the sentences are short and snappy
  - why the sentences use the present tense.
- Display an enlarged version of photocopiable page 33 and together with the learners read the instructions for how to play 'Hoopla'.

- Take the class outside and use the instructions to play 'Hoopla'. Ask: *Were the instructions easy to follow?*
- Next give each group a large ball and a skipping rope and ask them to create a new game to be played in a similar way. Encourage them to listen to each other's ideas and try out different suggestions until they agree on a new game.
- Ask each group to rehearse their new game, before demonstrating it to the other groups. Can they think of a good name for their game?
- When all the groups have demonstrated their games, ask the learners to choose one to play as a class.
- Give each learner photocopiable page 33 and ask them to complete the instructions for the class's chosen game.

Plenary

- Make copies of the instructions for both games ('Hoopla' and the class's chosen game), cut them up into strips and muddle them up into one pile.
- Organise the learners into small groups and give each small group a set of muddled instructions, two pieces of paper and some glue.
- Tell the groups to work as a team to re-assemble the two sets of instructions and glue them down on separate pieces of paper. The first team to finish wins.

Success criteria

Ask the learners:

- Why do instructions need a title?
- How are instructions set out on the page?
- What tense are instructions written in?

Ideas for differentiation

Support: Ask these learners to demonstrate their new game and then model how to write this in a template like the one on photocopiable page 33.

Extension: Ask these learners to create a poster of what must be found in a set of instructions.

Name: _____

Hoopla

You will need:

Beanbags, hoops.

What to do

1. Divide the players into equal teams, standing in lines.

2. Place a hoop a short distance away from each team and give the first player in each team a beanbag.

3. On 'Go', the first player in each team must throw the beanbag into the hoop, run and get it and give it to the next player, then run to the back of the line.

4. The next player must then throw the beanbag into the hoop, and so on.

5. When everyone in the team has had a turn throwing the beanbag and the first player is back at the front, the whole team should sit down. The winning team is the first to sit down.

Think of a new team game using a large ball, instead of hoops and beanbags, and use this frame to write the instructions.

Title:
You will need:
What to do   1. Divide class into teams of equal numbers.   2. Stand teams in lines, one behind the other.   3. _____   _____   4. _____   _____

Plastic bottles

Learning objectives

- Read and follow simple instructions, e.g. in a recipe. (2Rx2)
- Identify general features of known text types. (2Rv2)
- Articulate clearly so that others can hear. (2SL3)

Resources

Photocopiable page 35; three plastic bottles, each half filled with water, for each group of six learners; chalk; large lightweight balls; a range of hoops, beanbags, and so on.

Starter

- Play 'Plastic bottles' (see photocopiable page 35).
- Model how to play this game with a group of six learners.
- Now ask the learners to set up this game in groups, then play it a few times. Ensure that all the learners understand how the game is played.

Main activities

- Hand out individual copies of photocopiable page 35. Ask the learners to read the instructions for the game in their group then to draw an annotated diagram for the game on the back of their photocopiable page. Encourage them to share ideas amongst themselves.
- When they've finished, ask them to answer the questions on the photocopiable page. This should help them consolidate their knowledge of the features of instructions.
- In their groups, ask the learners to discuss what they liked best about the game and whether they would teach it to a friend.

- Ask them to work in pairs to create a new game that can be played with water bottles, drawing diagrams to illustrate the game. Provide access to a number of bottles, balls and other equipment for them to try out ideas with. Suggest other ideas to get them thinking, for example:
  - place the bottles in a long line quite close together and dodge in and out of them, trying not to knock any over
  - place the bottles in a line and try to knock them over with a beanbag
  - place the bottles in a group and try to throw a hoop over them without knocking them over
  - create an obstacle course that requires the players to jump over the bottles.

Plenary

- Play a game of skittles with the learners (using nine half-filled water bottles). Give each player three goes to knock down the skittles, capturing their total on a score board.
- Together with the learners, as a piece of shared writing, write a set of instructions for playing skittles.

Success criteria

Ask the learners:

- What is the purpose of instructions?
- What makes instructions easy to follow?
- Tell me the key features of instructions.

Ideas for differentiation

Support: Invite more-able learners to work with these learners, helping them to read the questions and advising on their pictures.

Extension: Ask these learners to create a set of instructions for a different game using a skipping rope, trying out and testing ideas before they write it.

Name: _____

Plastic bottles

For two or more players.

The aim: knock down all three bottles before the defender can stand them back up.

You will need:

Chalk, three plastic bottles each half full of water, a large lightweight ball.

What to do

1. Draw a circle on the ground with chalk (about 2 m wide) and pick one player to be the Defender.

2. The Defender must put the three bottles in the centre of the circle and stand there to defend them.

3. All of the other players must stand outside the circle and take turns rolling the ball at the bottles.

4. The Defender must block the ball with their feet and legs.

5. If a bottle falls, the Defender can stand it up again.

6. Whoever knocks down all three bottles in one go, before they can be stood up again, is the next Defender.

Instructions checklist	✓ or ✗
Does it have a title?	
Does it tell you how many people can play the game?	
Does it tell you what you need to play the game?	
Are the instructions easy to follow?	
Does it have short, snappy sentences?	
Does it have bossy words?	
Is it written in the present tense?	

Hopscotch

Learning objectives

- Identify general features of known text types. (2Rv2)
- Listen carefully and respond appropriately, asking questions of others. (2SL7)
- Show awareness of the listener by including relevant details. (2SL5)

Resources

Internet access; photocopiable page 37; chalk; a puppet.

Starter

- Tell the learners that they will play three hopscotch games outside and organise the instructions for one game.
- Watch instructions for playing hopscotch on the internet (for example at www.youtube.com/watch?v=fZzswQaICfM or www.videojug.com/film/how-to-play-hopscotch). Ask the learners to listen carefully so they can explain to others how to play.
- Ask them to turn to a partner and talk through these instructions.
- They can now go outside and draw the grid and then play the game.
- Check if they are all following the rules of the game!

Main activities

- Play traditional hopscotch, using a marker and hopping through the grid.
- Without using a marker, ask the learners to hop through the grid and back again. If they complete the grid successfully they should remain in the game and go to the back of the line; if the learner loses their balance or puts a foot wrong they are out. The winner is the last player left in.

- Organise the learners into groups outside and ask each group to draw a snail grid and a snake grid on the playground. Ask them to test out both games on both grids before choosing a grid and a game to play a second time.
- Back in the classroom, hand out individual copies of photocopiable page 37 and ask the learners to cut out and reorder the instructions on the page.

Plenary

- In front of the whole class, draw a hopscotch grid on the floor.
- Show the learners your puppet. Tell them that the puppet is going to tell them how to play hopscotch and that they have to listen carefully and raise their hands when he gets something wrong.
- Using the puppet, give the instructions for playing hopscotch. Make some deliberate mistakes and wait for the learners to correct you.

Success criteria

Ask the learners:

- How do you draw a hopscotch grid?
- Were the instructions for hopscotch clear enough on the film?
- Can you say how to play hopscotch?
- What are the rules of hopscotch?

Ideas for differentiation

Support: Ask these learners to draw a ladybird outline in the playground, dividing the back into segments, each with a spot in the middle. Challenge them to play hopscotch by throwing a stone or beanbag into each segment in turn and jumping into each square without placing their feet on the lines of the segments.

Extension: Ask these learners to create their own hopscotch grid and devise a game for it, trying out and agreeing choices between themselves before writing a set of instructions with diagrams.

Hopscotch

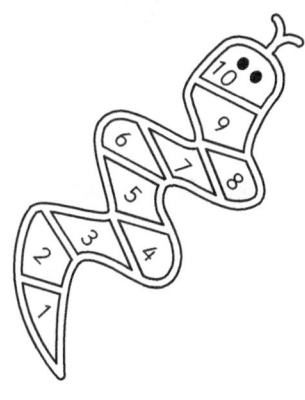

Cut out the instructions below and sort them into the right order to create a set of instructions for playing hopscotch.

Now continue as before, sliding or throwing your marker into the next square.

Jump over the first square, landing exactly in the next one – if you step on a line your go is over.

Aim: To be the first player to hop through the grid following the pattern.

When you make a mistake and your go is finished, go to the back of the queue. At your next go, start at the level you were at last time.

Draw a hopscotch pattern on the ground and number each square in order.

Stand at the beginning and throw or slide your marker into the first square – if it lands on a line or outside, your go is over.

How to play:

Pick up your marker and hop into each square until you finish.

Give each player a marker such as a stone or a shell.

Number of players: two or more.

Hyena race

- Read and follow simple instructions, e.g. in a recipe. (2Rx2)
- Find answers to questions by reading a section of text. (2Rx3)
- Show some awareness that texts have different purposes. (2Rv1)

Resources

Photocopiable page 39; counters and dice; pictures of a hyena and African women carrying water on their heads.

Starter

- Tell the learners that they are going to learn to play a game called 'Hyena race' and that spiral games like this one have been played in Africa for thousands of years! This game comes from Somalia, a country in Africa. Show pictures of a hyena and explain that it is a very good hunter. Show images of African women carrying water and discuss the lack of running water in African huts.
- Hand out enlarged versions of photocopiable page 39, one between two learners, and ask them to colour in their spiral using a sequence of colours for the squares to make it more attractive. If possible, cut out and laminate the spirals.

Main activities

- Read the instructions on photocopiable page 39 together with the learners, asking:
  - *What will you need to play the game?*
  - *What is a counter?*
  - *What is a dice?*
- Tell them that one counter is called 'mother' because, like a mother who needs water for cooking, washing and drinking, it moves to and from the well to get water.

- After reading the instructions, check that the learners can explain the rules of the game.
- Tell them that these instructions look slightly different from the ones they have seen so far – but bossy words are still there.
- Ask them to underline any bossy words they can find ('place', 'take', 'move', 'throw', and so on).
- Ask the learners in groups of four to six to play the game. Move around the groups, checking they are playing it correctly.

Plenary

- Ask the learners to turn to a partner to explain the rules of the game.
- Ask them to think about why the hyena counter can move twice as fast across the spiral.
- Ask them to think about the purpose of this game (to have fun with friends, to learn how to be a good loser, for example if you get eaten up by the hyena and have to stop playing).

Success criteria

Ask the learners:

- If six children are playing, how many counters will you need?
- Where is the mother counter aiming to go?
- What is the danger that might happen to your mother counter if it hasn't reached home safely?
- What do you think the purpose of this game is?

Ideas for differentiation

Support: Ensure that these learners are in mixed-ability groups so that they can play the game successfully.

Extension: Ask these learners to re-write the rules so that they are shorter than the ones on photocopiable page 39.

Name: _____

Hyena race

You will need:

Two different-coloured counters for each player (one for 'mother' who is off to get water, the other for a hungry hyena), a dice.

What to do

1. Place your mother counter on the first square. Throw the dice and move the counter the number of spaces shown.

2. When you reach the well, throw a six before moving back home.

3. When home, take a hyena counter and start again. This time, move twice the number of squares shown on the dice.

4. If you jump over a mother counter, take it off the board – it has been 'eaten'!

5. Continue until all the players have made it back to the village or been eaten.

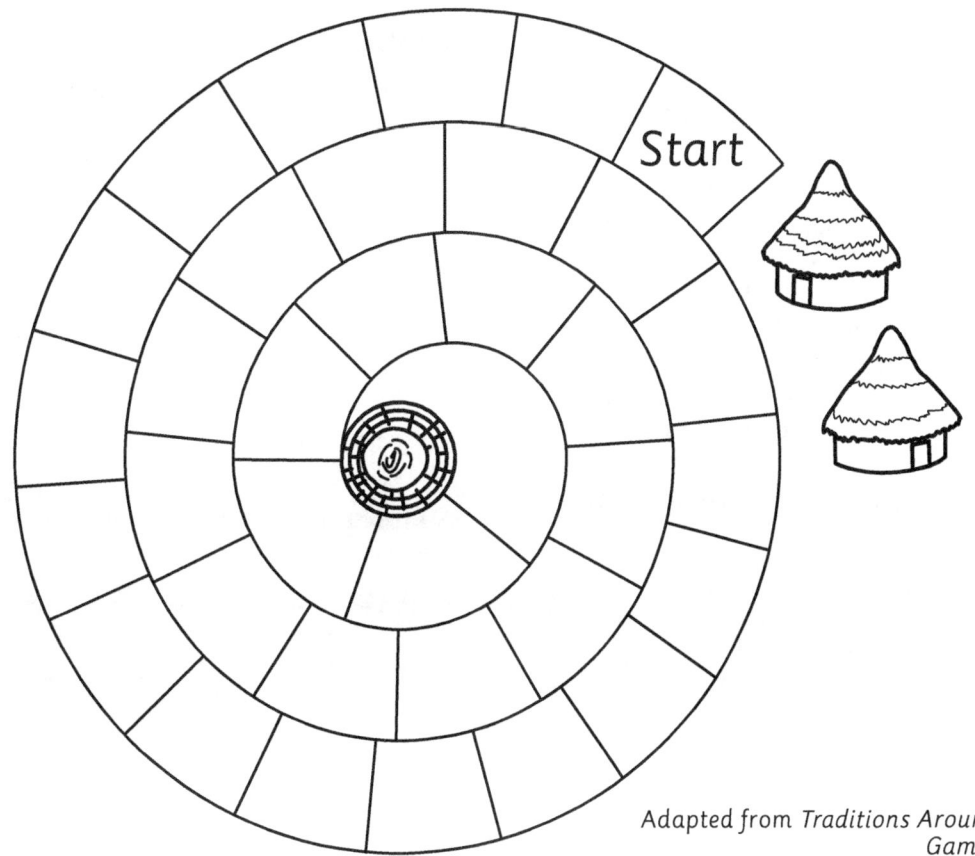

Adapted from *Traditions Around The World: Games* (Wayland)

Making a board game

- Write instructions and recount events and experiences. (2Wa6)
- Use features of chosen text type. (2Wa5)
- Explain plans and ideas, extending them in the light of discussion. (2SL2)

Resources

Photocopiable page 41; different-coloured A4 card cut in half; heavy A3 card; felt-tipped pens, glue sticks; dice and counters.

Starter

- Tell the learners that they are going to make their own board game and write instructions to go with it.
- Organise the learners into groups of four and give each learner half a piece of different-coloured A4 card, and each group one piece of heavier weight A3 card.
- Ask each learner first to measure and cut off three 3 cm-wide strips from the long side of their A4 page.
- Then ask them to cut these strips into small squares of 3 cm × 3 cm.
- Ask them to place these squares along all four edges of the A3 card, agreeing on a colour sequence. When they've finished the edges they should spiral in until their squares run out.
- Ask them to write the word START on a square at one corner of the track, then number the next square 1 and continue until they reach the last square in the sequence and write the word FINISH.
- Tell them to mark every fifth card with a black spot.

START	1	2	3	4
●	16	17	18	●
14	FINISH		19	6
13	22	21	●	7
12	11	●	9	8

Main activities

- Hand out two copies of photocopiable page 41 to each group and ask them to cut out the cards, shuffle them and place them in a pile in the centre of their board.
- Provide the groups with a dice and four different-coloured counters. Tell the learners to start playing their game by taking turns to throw the dice and move their counter. If they land on a square with a black spot, they should pick up a card and carry out the instructions.
- The first one to reach FINISH is the winner.

Plenary

- Ask the learners to think of a name for this game and write up the favourite on a screen or board.
- Then ask them to tell you what is needed to play the game, and how to play it, writing what they say and checking it makes sense as you go along.
- Challenge the learners to think of a few new ideas for the cards!

Success criteria

Ask the learners:

- Tell me what you will do with your coloured paper.
- What colour sequence did you choose?
- Why do you need a START and a FINISH square?
- Which game card made you laugh?
- Did the cards work well in your team?

Ideas for differentiation

Support: Have some ready-made game cards for these learners to use.

Extension: Ask these learners to make up another board game, but create a different basic shape and draw pictures around it and at the start and finish. This could be linked to a favourite topic, for example pirates or a magic castle. They could make game cards to match the new theme.

Board-game cards

Cut out these cards and place them in the centre of your game board.

START	1	2	3	4
•	16	17	18	•
14	FINISH		19	6
13	22	21	•	7
12	11	•	9	8

Your favourite programme is on TV – miss a turn.	You've eaten all your vegetables – move forward three spaces.	You've forgotten your PE kit – go back three spaces.
You were late for school – go back two spaces.	You're too tired to move – stay where you are.	You've got to do your homework – stay where you are.
All your spellings were correct – move forward five spaces.	You stayed up late – go back four spaces.	Ice cream for tea! Run to the finish!
Swap places with another player.	You fell off the trampoline – go back six spaces.	You've slipped on a banana skin – go back one space.

TV presentation

Learning objectives

- Read and follow simple instructions, e.g. in a recipe. (2Rx2)
- Extend experiences and ideas through role-play. (2SL9)
- Articulate clearly so that others can hear. (2SL3)

Resources

Photocopiable page 43; card or thick paper; black wax crayons; brightly-coloured wax crayons; plastic knives, paintbrushes or ice-lolly sticks.

Starter

- Tell the learners that they are going to make a wax picture as a gift for a friend.
- Hand out individual copies of photocopiable page 43 and ask the learners to read and discuss the instructions with a partner.
- Move around and check that all the learners are clear about how to make this present.

Main activities

- Explain to the learners that they will work in groups to create a pretend TV show in which they will demonstrate how to create the picture. Organise the pairs into groups of six.
- Display a format for the TV demonstration on the board, for example:
  - First learner as TV host: 'Welcome to our show! Today we are going to …'
  - Second learner: 'You will need …'
  - Third learner: 'First you need to …'
  - Fourth learner: 'Next …'
  - Fifth learner: 'Finally …'
  - Sixth learner: 'Here are some …'
- Talk through the format, giving advice and modelling what the learners could say:
  - The TV host and all the learners must speak in lively, interesting ways: 'Welcome to our show! Today we are going to show you how to make a dramatic wax picture.'
- The second learner should take enough time to show and describe what is needed: 'You will need some brightly coloured wax crayons …'
- The third, fourth and fifth learners need to clearly explain and show how to make the pictures: 'First you need to draw a really colourful background. You could use a bold stripe or zig-zag pattern. Next you need to cover all the colour with thick black crayon. Finally you need to scratch off the wax with a plastic knife or …'
- The sixth learner needs to show some completed pictures: 'Here are some pictures we made earlier …'
- Have all the materials arranged on a table for each group and ask them to rehearse their presentation.
- Discuss what props they might need. Do they have time to do a whole picture for the demonstration or do they want to show the start of each stage and hold up a completed version of each stage?

Plenary

- Ask one of the groups to perform their TV demonstration and the rest of the class to comment on the presentation. Ask: *How easy was it to follow the instructions? How clearly did the presenters speak? How interesting was it to listen to?*

Success criteria

Ask the learners:

- If you don't understand anything when reading instructions, what should you do?
- Why do you need to speak clearly when you are showing others what to do?
- Why is it important to smile and show you are enjoying yourself when doing a presentation?

Ideas for differentiation

Support: Ensure that these learners take a full and active part, working with mixed-ability groups.

Extension: Ask these learners to organise their group to ensure everyone is involved and they are all helping each other with their lines.

How to make a wax picture

You will need:

Card or thick paper, black wax crayons, brightly-coloured wax crayons, plastic knives or paintbrushes or ice-lolly sticks.

What to do

1. Draw a bold pattern in brightly-coloured wax crayons on a sheet of paper – you can use stripes, circles or any other shapes. Completely cover the paper.

2. Cover the coloured pattern with thick black wax. Make sure that the colours are completely covered.

3. Scratch out a picture in the black wax using a plastic knife, a lolly stick or the end of a paintbrush, exposing the colours beneath.

Whirling, shooting and exploding fireworks make a colourful picture! Or you could scratch off a flower, a fairy castle or a strange alien from another planet!

Making a paper flower

Learning objectives

● Read and follow simple instructions, e.g. in a recipe. (2Rx2)

● Read and respond to question words, e.g. *what, where, when, who, why*. (2Rx1)

● Articulate clearly so that others can hear. (2SL3)

Resources

Photocopiable pages 35 and 45; sheets of kitchen towel; coloured tissue paper; felt-tipped pens; bendable straws; sticky tape; scissors; yellow paper or yellow wool.

Starter

• Tell the learners that they are going to learn how to make paper flowers as a gift for a parent or carer.

• Hand out photocopiable page 45 and ask the learners to read the instructions in pairs.

• When they have finished reading, ask them to join another pair of learners.

• As a group of four learners, they must all contribute to a discussion about how to make paper flowers. Encourage them to listen carefully to other group members, asking questions if they wish.

Main activities

• Display these questions about the instructions and ask the learners to read and respond to them in the same small groups of four:
  • What helped you read the instructions in the right order? (Numbers.)
  • Why are there pictures in these instructions? (To make the instructions clear.)
  • Which bossy words are used? ('Fold', 'Draw', 'Make'.)
  • Why are these bossy words so good? (They tell you exactly what to do.)

• Call the class back together and share their responses to these questions, encouraging them to speak clearly so that others can hear.

• Have the materials for making the flowers available and ask the learners to collect what they need and to make several flowers to create a bunch to take home.

• Hand out photocopiable page 35 and ask the learners to fill in the evaluation section for this set of instructions.

• Create a display of the instructions, evaluations and paper flowers.

Plenary

• In pairs, ask the learners:
  • *What was missing from these instructions?*
  • *What did the instructions have that helped you to make these flowers easily?*
  • *Were the instructions short, snappy and clear?*

Success criteria

Ask the learners:

● What sort of verbs might you find in a set of instructions?

● What should you do first when you are about to follow a set of instructions?

● How do diagrams help in a set of instructions?

● Why is it important to speak clearly when asking a question?

● Why is it important to speak clearly when answering a question?

Ideas for differentiation

Support: Ensure that these learners take a full and active part, working in mixed-ability groups.

Extension: Challenge these learners to make flowers out of a material of their choice but using circular pieces. When they have worked out what to do, ask them to write a set of instructions for the other learners to try out.

How to make paper flowers

1. Fold a sheet of kitchen towel in half. Open it out and cut along the fold.

2. Take one of the halves and fold it in half, long sides together.

3. Draw lots of stripes or other patterns along the paper with a felt-tipped pen.

4. Fold in half with the short sides together, then fold in half again.

5. Make long cuts close together from the bottom. Don't cut all the way up.

6. Open it carefully, so that it looks like this.

7. Tape one end of the paper onto to a bendable straw. Roll the paper tightly around it and fasten the loose end with tape.

8. Pull all the petals down.

9. Snip up little pieces of yellow paper or wool and glue these to the centre of your flower.

10. Repeat with the other half of kitchen towel to make another flower.

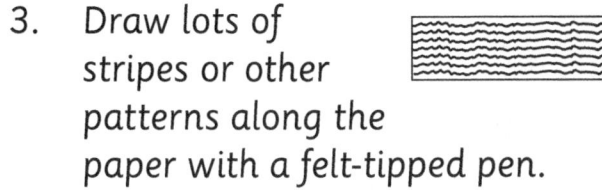

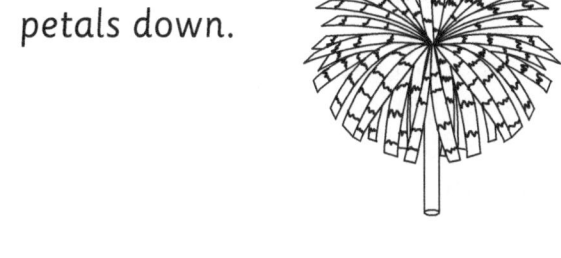

Adapted from **What Shall I Do Today?** (Usborne)

Paper penguins

Learning objectives

- Explain plans and ideas, extending them in the light of discussion. (2SL2)
- Articulate clearly so that others can hear. (2SL3)
- Write instructions and recount events and experiences. (2Wa6)

Resources

Photocopiable page 47; a finished penguin for each group; black and white card; orange card or orange paint; glue; scissors; rulers.

Starter

- Before the lesson prepare some penguins, using the template on photocopiable page 47 and different-coloured card.
- Tell the learners that you are giving them a challenge today! They are going to have to work out how to make something from the finished product.
- Show them a completed penguin but don't give them any clues as to how it has been made. Tell them that penguins live together in huge colonies so they must all make one! You want the penguins they make to be the same size as the ones you have made.

Main activities

- Divide the class into small groups of mixed-ability learners.
- Give each group a completed penguin and a ruler.
- Circulate as they discuss how it was made, encouraging them to speak clearly and explain to each other how it must have been made.
- Have the materials available and ask the learners to select the materials they will need to make their own penguin.

- When everyone has finished a penguin, tell the group to discuss what information needs to go in a set of instructions for making one. Hand out individual copies of photocopiable page 47, and ask the learners to continue to discuss their instructions: *What goes first? What language will you use?* When they are confident, ask them to write their own version, discussing the task and supporting each other as they write.
- Encourage them to read their instructions aloud to each other at different stages. *Have they missed anything out? Is the language clear and bossy?*
- When they've finished, choose different group members to talk through the process of making their penguin. Ask: *Did anyone else refer to the picture to help their reader? Did anyone suggest that their reader use the penguin picture as a template?*

Plenary

- Ask all the learners to talk about:
  - what was easy and what was difficult about this task
  - how they worked as a team
  - how they planned what to write together.

Success criteria

Ask the learners:

- Which part of the penguin do you need to make first?
- Which smaller parts do you need?
- How can you make sure that it will be the same size?
- Why do you need to write clear instructions?
- Explain what you did at each stage of making the penguin.

Ideas for differentiation

Support: Encourage other learners in the mixed-ability groups to help these learners to make the penguin and write the instructions.

Extension: Ask these learners to organise a presentation on how to make a penguin, following the plan on making wax pictures on photocopiable page 43.

Name: _____

How to make a penguin

Use this frame to write a set of instructions for making a penguin.

You will need:

_____

_____

_____

_____

What to do

1. _____

2. _____

3. _____

4. _____

5. _____

6. _____

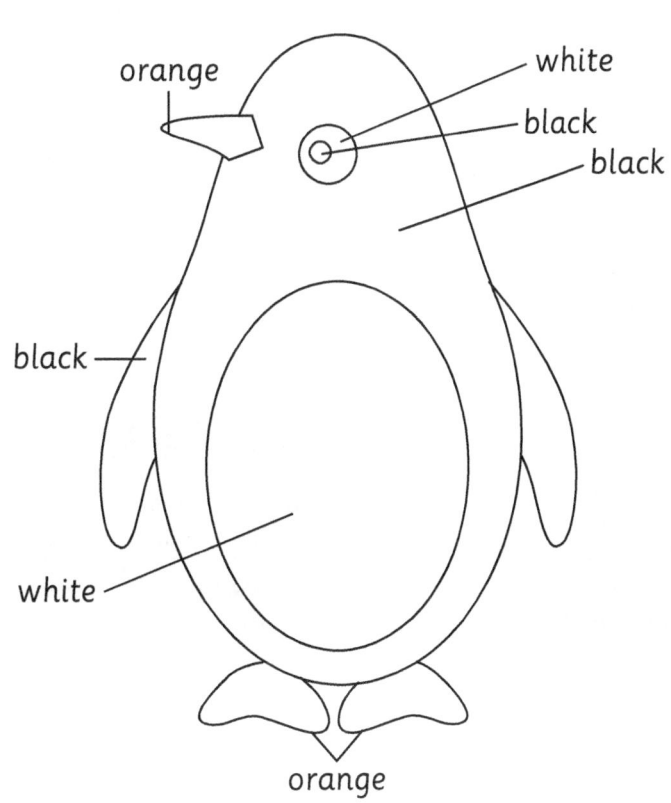

Sweet and spicy popcorn

Learning objectives

● Identify general features of known text types. (2Rv2)

● Begin to re-read own writing aloud to check for sense and accuracy. (2W03)

● Demonstrate 'attentive listening' and engage with another speaker. (2SL8)

Resources

Internet access; photocopiable page 49; sugar, chilli powder, ground cinnamon, salt, cayenne pepper, six cups of plain popped popcorn, non-stick olive oil cooking spray; zip-type plastic bag; large pieces of paper.

Starter

• Watch popcorn being popped on the internet, or join in singing and dancing with a popcorn song (for example at www.youtube.com/watch?v=bo3YbmhkEcM).

Main activities

• Tell the learners that you have been shopping and that you have the ingredients for a delicious popcorn recipe: Sweet and spicy popcorn!

• Take out the ingredients one by one, and tell the learners what they are.

• Ask them to write down the headings: 'Title', 'Ingredients' and 'What to do'. Tell them that when you show them the recipe, they should make notes under each heading because later they will write this recipe down. Remind them that to take notes they just need to write key words, not everything you say.

• Make the popcorn using the recipe on photocopiable page 49. Talk the learners through every stage, giving them time to make notes and giving advice on the note-making process as you go, for example: *Remember to write the name of each ingredient. Don't forget to write the correct quantity – 1 tablespoon of sugar and a pinch of cayenne pepper.*

• Divide the learners into groups and ask them to write this recipe down together on a large piece of paper.

• Move around the groups of learners, encouraging them to share the task, listening carefully to what the other learners are suggesting, re-reading what they have written, checking for sense and accuracy.

• Hand out photocopiable page 49 to each group and ask them to use it to evaluate their shared recipe.

• Collect these in and praise those who have scored well – but give all the learners a taste of the sweet and spicy popcorn! (Check for food allergies first.)

Plenary

• Show the learners a set of ingredients: chocolate chips, cooked popcorn, salt and melted butter, and ask groups to make up a recipe, writing it down on a large piece of paper.

• Ask them to tell you what made it difficult. (Working out the quantity of ingredients?)

Success criteria

Ask the learners:

● Why do recipes have names or titles at the top?

● Why are ingredients listed in a particular order?

● Why is the exact quantity needed?

● Why are bossy words used?

● Why are the sentences short?

● Which tense is used?

Ideas for differentiation

Support: Give these learners a cut-up version of photocopiable page 49 for them to put back together with the assistance of an adult helper.

Extension: Ask these learners to write instructions for a popcorn popping dance!

Name: _____

Sweet and spicy popcorn

	Did you include this in your recipe? ✓ or ✗
Title: Sweet and Spicy Popcorn	
Ingredients	
1 tablespoon sugar	
$\frac{1}{2}$ teaspoon ground cinnamon	
$\frac{1}{4}$ teaspoon salt	
pinch cayenne pepper	
6 cups plain popped popcorn	
Non-stick olive oil cooking spray	
What to do	
Place sugar, cinnamon, salt and cayenne pepper in a large zip-type plastic bag.	
Shake to mix the ingredients together.	
Add the popcorn.	
Spray the popcorn with non-stick olive oil cooking spray.	
Close the bag and shake.	
Spray and shake twice more until the popcorn is covered.	

'The sandwich'

Learning objectives

- Read aloud with increased accuracy, fluency and expression. (2R06)
- Use phonics as the main method of tackling unfamiliar words. (2R02)
- Use features of chosen text type. (2Wa5)

Resources

Photocopiable page 51; large pieces of paper; coloured card, tissue paper and a range of craft materials; scissors; glue.

Starter

- Ask selected learners to read 'The sandwich' by Tony Bradman on photocopiable page 51 with expression. Define any unfamiliar words, for example 'slap' – spread, 'marge' – margarine, 'bung' – put, add, and so on.

Main activities

- Write 'The sandwich', 'Ingredients' and 'Method' on the board.
- Hand out photocopiable page 51 and ask the learners to re-read the poem in pairs. Ask them to tell you the list of ingredients in the order in which they appear. Write these on a long piece of paper, and stick this under the heading 'Ingredients'.
- Under 'Method', model turning the second verse into an instruction: 'Take two slices of bread and spread them with jam and margarine'.
- Divide the learners into five groups and give each group a verse from 3 to 7 to convert into instructions. Ask them to discuss it first before writing it down on a piece of paper.
- Move around the groups, asking them which bossy words they've used.
- Stick the instructions in order under 'Take two slices …'

- Explain that as a class you're going to make this sandwich … out of craft materials. Ask the groups to make the ingredients from their verse. Provide a large range of paper, wool, string and other craft materials. Ask the learners to make sure that each ingredient is at least 40 cm long in order to make a towering sandwich for a display! Ask those who finish first to make some 'jam and marge'.
- Lay a large piece of paper on the floor and read out the completed recipe as the learners place their ingredients on the sandwich. Top it off with a final piece of paper.

Plenary

- Make up a silly soup recipe. Ask the learners to get into groups, think of silly things to put into a soup and write a list.
- Organise cookery demonstrations for the learners, where each group must say the name of their soup (for example 'Super spidery soup') and mime how to make it.

Success criteria

Ask the learners:

- What will be the title for this recipe?
- How would you sound out this word?
- How will you make the sandwich?
- Which are the bossy words?
- Which is more fun to read, the poem or the recipe?

Ideas for differentiation

Support: Ask these learners to make the first and last pieces of bread, then be the team in charge of sticking all the ingredients in the right order, with an adult helper to support them.

Extension: Ask these learners to be extreme with their silly soup recipe. How revolting can it be? Ask them to write their recipe down.

The sandwich

Oh what shall I have
Today for my tea?
I know – a sandwich,
As big as can be!

I'll start with the bread,
Two slices, quite large;
Then slap on some jam,
Oh yes, and some marge,

I'll put in some cheese,
A tomato or two,
And maybe an onion
This big one will do!

I'll bung in some lettuce,
A radish, of course,
And ... a sizzling burger,
All covered in sauce!

Add in some chicken,
And maybe some chips,
Some biscuits, an apple,
A packet of crisps,

A cake with some candles,
Some chocolate (one bar),
Spaghetti, bananas,
Sweets from a jar,

Baked beans and humbugs,
Carrots and mustard,
All topped off with cream
And steaming hot custard ...

Now a sandwich like that
You really can't beat,
It's packed out with goodies.
A real tasty treat.

There's only one problem;
It's breaking my heart ...
It's such a big sandwich –
Where do I start?

Tony Bradman

Recipes for a special person

Learning objectives

- Extend experiences and ideas through role-play. (2SL9)
- Write instructions and recount events and experiences. (2Wa6)
- Demonstrate 'attentive listening' and engage with another speaker. (2SL8)

Starter

- Tell the learners they are going to make a recipe to show how to keep their mum, dad or another special person happy!
- Go into role as a mum and ask the learners to ask you about things that you wished your children would do, for example clean their teeth, not interrupt when you are talking to a friend, give you lots of hugs, and so on.

Main activities

- Now ask the learners to write lists of things that would make their special person very pleased.
- Move around the class, reading the lists and giving feedback to the learners.
- Write up some of the things they have written and tell them that these will be part of the 'Method' for their recipe. Explain that each instruction must start with a bossy word.
- Ask what the title of this recipe could be, for example 'Keeping Mum happy'.
- Ask them what the main ingredient would be – what would make them want to do nice things for their Mum? Because they love her a lot?
- Combine these elements to create a recipe, for example:

> **Keeping Mum happy**
> **Ingredients**
> Lots of love and care
> **Method**
> 1. Make my bed every day.
> 2. Clear the table.

- Hand out photocopiable page 53 to each learner. Ask them to choose who they are going to write their recipe about. Ask them to then write their recipe in the middle of the page and draw pictures of the kind things that they would do for the person around the edge.
- Call the class together and ask them to read out their recipes.
- Create a class book of recipes called 'Keeping everyone happy'.

Plenary

- Ask small groups of learners to think what might go in the 'Method' section of a recipe for 'Keeping our teacher happy'.
- Ask each group to write two ideas on large strips of paper, each one starting with a bossy word, for example: 'Spell words correctly.', 'Listen carefully.'
- Stick all the ideas under the word 'Method' and talk about what has been written; add a title and a list of ingredients (eager mind, good attitude, listening ears).

Success criteria

Ask the learners:

- Which ideas did 'Mum' give you in the Starter session?
- Why were the instructions for 'Keeping Mum happy' written in the same way as for any set of instructions?
- Why is it important to listen very carefully when someone is explaining things to you?

Ideas for differentiation

Support: Provide writing support for these learners.

Extension: Challenge these learners to add rhyme to their recipe to turn it into a poem.

Name: _____

Keeping a special person happy

Write a recipe for keeping someone important in your life happy.
Draw pictures of what you have written about in your recipe.

Title: _____

Ingredients

_____

_____

Method

1. _____

2. _____

3. _____

4. _____

5. _____

6. _____

7. _____

8. _____

Unit assessment

Questions to ask

- How do instructions look different from stories?
- Which headings will you always find in instructions?
- Why do instructions always tell you what you need?

- Why are bossy words used?
- Why do instructions use short, snappy sentences?
- Is a recipe a set of instructions?

Summative assessment activities

Observe the learners while they play these games. You will quickly be able to identify those who appear to be confident and those who may need additional support.

Which game?

This is a useful activity to assess if the learners remember the types of instructions used for different activities.

You will need:

Cut-out instruction sentences from the hopscotch game on photocopiable page 37 and the popcorn recipe on photocopiable page 49; two hoops, one labelled 'Hopscotch' and the other 'Sweet and spicy popcorn'.

What to do

- Give each pair of learners a set of sentences from each set of instructions ('Sweet and spicy popcorn' recipe and 'Hopscotch').
- Ask them to sort these into two separate sets of instructions when you say 'Go', then run and place these in the correct hoop.
- Check if these are correct by reading out a selection of sentences and ask the class to say if they think it is correct or incorrect.

How to make it

This game ensures that the learners can match the right ingredients to the title of a recipe.

You will need:

Photocopiable page 55.

What to do

- Cut up the grid up on photocopiable page 55 and give each learner a set of the two lists of ingredients.
- Ask the learners to sort these ingredients under the correct recipe name.
- Give them a maximum time of five minutes, then check that these have been sorted correctly.

Written assessment

Hand out individual copies of photocopiable page 55 and ask the learners to create a recipe of their choice using the ingredients.

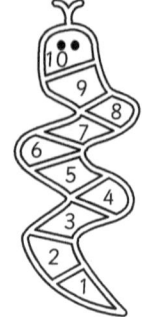

Name: _____

Which recipe?

Salad on a plate	Berry popcorn
tomatoes	cooked popcorn
cucumber	blueberries
onions	sugar
mayonnaise	yoghurt

Choose one of the titles and list of ingredients above and write the recipe below. To help you, the ingredients above are in the correct order!

Title: _____

Ingredients:

_____

_____

_____

_____

What to do

1. _____

2. _____

3. _____

4. _____

Unit 1C: Poems in familiar settings

Playground rhymes

Learning objectives

- Read poems and comment on words and sounds, rhyme and rhythm. (2Rw3)
- Use the structures of familiar poems and stories in developing own writing. (2W05)
- Extend experiences and ideas through role-play. (2SL9)

Resources

Photocopiable page 57; hoops; camera.

Starter

- Take the learners into a large space where they can run around.
- Place a number of hoops on the ground – enough hoops for one between two or three learners.
- Tell them that when they hear you shout 'Puddle', they must all shout 'Puddle!' and run and jump into a hoop, calling out 'Splash!'
- Learn the poem below by heart together with the learners and create some actions. Film the result.

The playtime puddle rhyme
Puddle, splash, puddle, splash,
Don't go near the puddle, splash.
You'll get into trouble, splash,
So don't go near the puddle – SPLASH!

Mike Jubb

Main activities

- Staying in the large area, display and read an enlarged version of 'You can't catch me!' by John Foster on photocopiable page 57.
- Ask four learners to come to the front and stand in a circle, all facing in a clockwise direction.
- Ask these learners to chase each other round in a circle. Create a verse using the format of John Foster's poem using their names (one will have to be 'me').

- Say the verse aloud as they run, encouraging all the learners to join in, for example:

I chased Amelie.
Amelie chased Tia.
Tia chased Lian.
Lian chased me.

- Then ask them to stop and chase each other in reverse order, saying the new verse.
- Ask the whole class to get into circles of four and re-enact the poem with their names. Take photographs of them as they run.
- Back in the classroom, hand out individual copies of photocopiable page 57 and ask the learners to write their own first and third verses by using their friends' names.

Plenary

- Read the original poem together, clap out the rhythm and discuss the rhyme. Does anyone's new poem rhyme? Compare the rhythm of two or three new poems.
- Choose different groups of four to come to the front and say their verses as they chase each other.

Success criteria

Ask the learners:

- What did you enjoy about acting out 'The playtime puddle rhyme'?
- Why is John Foster's poem easy to learn?
- Did you have fun changing the 'chasing' poem to your friends' names?

Ideas for differentiation

Support: Ask these learners to make name cards and arrange them in a set of four in a circle. Then try out the game using one of the names as 'me' who starts off the chase!

Extension: Challenge these learners to use the names of the learners in the class to create a rhyming verse for the chasing poem.

Name: _____

You can't catch me!

I chased Tina.

Tina chased Lee.

Lee chased Pat.

Pat chased me.

In and out of the bushes.

Round and round the tree.

Up and down the path.

You can't catch me!

I chased Pat.

Pat chased Lee.

Lee chased Tina.

Tina chased me.

John Foster

1. Now write your own version of the poem on the back of this page. Write the names of the three friends who you chased in a circle in the first verse.

2. Do this again for the last verse, but remember that you are chasing them the other way around this time!

Poems about food

Starter

• Ask: *Who loves the smell of toast?* Display the poem 'Jam on toast' on photocopiable page 59 and read it together. Ask the learners if they have ever dropped their toast so that it fell face down and they couldn't eat it.

• How did it or would it make them feel?

• Read the poem again, emphasising the word 'always' in the last line.

• Display the poem 'One tongue' and ask the learners to read it and say what is funny about it.

• Ask them to draw two sad faces to show how the characters feel at the end of each poem.

Main activities

• Now read the poem 'Beans with everything' to the learners, reading the last line of each verse in an expressive way.

• Get the learners to join you in clapping the beat: 2/2/4 and copying the rhythm in your voice.

• Ask them to talk in pairs about whether they like baked beans and what they like to eat them with – and then to share this with the class.

• Ask them to think of some silly things to which beans could be added: 'Beans in a trifle / Beans in a mousse / Beans in lemonade / Beans in juice' (a trifle is a cold pudding made with fruit placed in a dish covered with custard and / or cream).

• Ask the learners to think of other foods that beans could be added to – silly or sensible – and to write these down. Encourage them to shape their ideas into a new verse for the poem.

• Learn this poem, and add it to your class book of 'Poems we know'.

Plenary

• Ask the learners which poem they prefer and why.

• Ask some of the learners to read out their new verse for the 'Beans' poem. Who has the 'yuckiest' verse?

• Read the three poems again and discuss the way the characters are speaking: frustrated, happy, enthusiastic, sad, disappointed, and so on.

Food poems

Jam on toast

Why is strawberry jam so red?

Why is toast so brown?

Why when I drop it on the floor

Is it always jam side down?

Gareth Owen

One tongue

One tongue, one lollipop

Lick, lick, lick.

One tongue, no more lollipop.

Just one stick.

Julia Donaldson

Beans with everything

Beans on bread,

Beans on toast;

Beans are what I love the most.

Beans in a pie,

Beans in a stew;

Beans are what I love to chew.

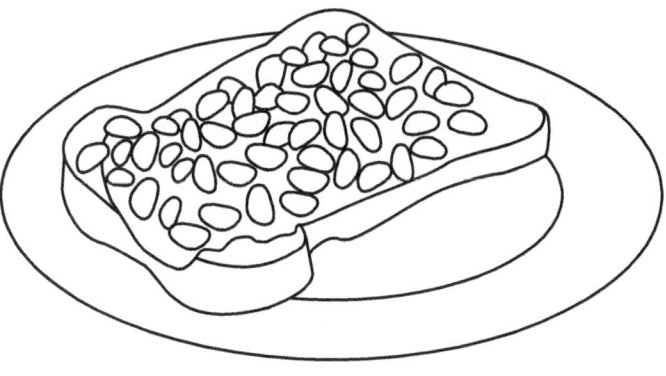

Beans and chips,

Beans and fish;

Beans are such a lovely dish.

Beans with veg,

Beans with meat;

Beans are what I want to eat.

Mike Jubb

Bedtime

Learning objectives

- Use the structures of familiar poems and stories in developing own writing. (2W05)
- Recount experiences and explore possibilities. (2SL1)
- Begin to be aware of ways in which speakers vary talk, e.g. the use of more formal vocabulary and tone of voice. (2SL10)

Resources

Photocopiable page 61.

Starter

- Ask: *Do you ever play up at bedtime, making excuses for not going to bed?*
- Read 'Bedtime, please!' on photocopiable page 61, pointing out that it is based on the nursery rhyme 'One, two, buckle my shoe'. Read it in a cross or frustrated voice, saying the word 'LATE' a little louder.
- Ask the learners:
  - *Who is speaking in this poem?* (Parent or other carer.)
  - *Why it is spoken in such a cross voice?* (The speaker is tired; the child needs sleep.)
  - *Why is it such a snappy rhythm with 2/4 beats?* (Shows impatience with the child perhaps; the speaker is rushed and cross, perhaps.)
- Discuss the different thoughts the learners have.
- Ask the learners to read the poem aloud with expression.

Main activities

- Read aloud 'Bedtime' from photocopiable page 61. Read it in a pleading or whining voice.
- Read it again and get the learners to join in, copying your tone.
- Count and clap the 8/7 syllable beat of the poem. Discuss the effect of the longer beat here, compared with the snappy rhythm of 'Bedtime, please!'. (The tone here is whining and drawn out; the child is delaying bedtime).

- Ask different learners to read lines from the poem in a whining voice – who can sound the most pleading?
- Hand out individual copies of photocopiable page 61 and ask the learners to write their own poem in the style of 'Bedtime'. If they are stuck, encourage them to discuss ideas with a partner.
- Learn both poems, and add them to your book of 'Poems we know'.

Plenary

- Write the following sentence opener on the board: 'Mum, I can't tidy my bedroom ...'
- Give the learners strips of paper and ask them to write as many completions for this sentence as they can, using a different strip for each idea.
- Then all come together and ask them for their strips of paper and decide with them which ones to use to help you make a new poem called 'Tidying my bedroom'.

Success criteria

Ask the learners:

- Why does 'Bedtime, please!' have such a short, snappy beat?
- Why does 'Bedtime' have a longer beat?
- Why is each poem spoken in a cross voice?
- What do you like about these poems?
- What do you dislike about these poems?

Ideas for differentiation

Support: Ask these learners to learn the first poem and practise saying it and then perform it to the class.

Extension: Ask these learners to write 'Tidying my bedroom' unaided.

Name: _____

Bedtime

Bedtime, please!

One, two,

off with that shoe!

Three, four,

socks on the floor!

Five, six,

no more tricks!

Seven, eight,

you are LATE!

Nine, ten,

I won't tell you again!

Judith Nicholls

Bedtime

Five minutes, five minutes more please!

Let me stay five minutes more!

Can't I just finish the castle

I'm building here on the floor?

Can't I just finish the story

I'm reading here in my book?

Can't I just finish this bead-chain –

It almost is finished, look!

Can't I just finish this game, please!

When a game's once begun

It's a pity never to find out

Whether you've lost or won.

Can't I just stay five minutes?

Well, can't I just stay four?

Three minutes then? Two minutes?

Can't I stay one minute more?

Eleanor Farjeon

Now write your own going-to-bed poem by giving three more excuses for not going to bed, for example:

Can't I just finish the puzzle
I'm making here on the floor?

Days out

- Read poems and comment on words and sounds, rhyme and rhythm. (2Rw3)
- Extend experiences and ideas through role-play. (2SL9)
- Recount experiences and explore possibilities. (2SL1)

Resources

Photocopiable page 63.

Starter

- Ask: *Have you ever been on a picnic? Where did you go? What was the weather like? Does anyone have a funny story to tell about a picnic that went wrong?* Allow time for the learners to contribute their experiences.
- Display an enlarged version of photocopiable page 63 and read 'The picnic' to the class. Ask: *How can waves 'curl' up the beach?*
- Ask volunteers to point out any rhyming words. Ask: *Does the 8/6 beat suit the poem?*
- Ask: *Was this a good picnic or a bad one? Why do you think this?* Ask the learners to give details with their answer.

Main activities

- Read 'Our family picnic' from photocopiable page 63 together with the learners.
- Explain the meaning of 'lugged', 'plagued', 'tormented' and the idiom in the last lines (people say something was 'no picnic' when it was difficult).
- Ask the learners whether this was a good picnic or a bad one, and to say why, again giving details. Discuss the humour in the poem: How many things went wrong? Ask: *Do we often find rain, bees and mosquitoes in the same place?*
- Ask the learners to identify the rhythm and rhyming words.

- Ask them to turn to a partner and come up with some funny ideas for what fun things the children might do next in the park and what might go wrong, for example they might go out in a pedal boat on the lake and capsize, climb a tree and fall out, and so on.
- Invite some of the learners to role-play being at this picnic and tell the class what they did next.
- Now ask the learners to work in groups to write a sequel for 'Our family picnic', starting with the line: 'My family went out to the cinema ...', and writing about a few things that went wrong, for example they lost the tickets, the film was too scary, the film was boring, they lost a brother or sister in the dark, and so on.

Plenary

- Share the groups' cinema poems.
- Hot-seat some of the learners (ask them to get in role) as children who went to each picnic and ask the rest of the class to ask them questions about the day.

Success criteria

Ask the learners:

- What precise information do the poets give us so that we could draw pictures to show what is happening?
- What do you like about these poems?
- Which poem was more fun to read?
- Which poem could be called 'The perfect day' and which one 'The terrible day'?

Ideas for differentiation

Support: Ask these learners to draw a picture to illustrate one of these poems.

Extension: Challenge these learners to write a polished version of 'Our family trip to the cinema', mimicking the rhythm and rhyme structure of the original poem.

Eating outdoors

The picnic

We brought a rug for sitting on,

Our lunch was in a box.

The sand was warm. We didn't wear

Hats or shoes or socks.

Waves came curling up the beach.

We waded. It was fun.

Our sandwiches were different kinds.

I dropped my jammy one.

Dorothy Aldis

Our family picnic

My family went out on a picnic.

We lugged all our stuff to the park.

As soon as we'd spread out our
  blanket

it promptly got rainy and dark.

And while we were watching our
  napkins

and plates blow away in the breeze,

we all got attacked by mosquitoes

and plagued and tormented by bees.

Our sodas were slurped up by insects.

Our burgers were eaten by ants

which, once they were done with
  our lunches,

decided to crawl up our pants.

We couldn't hold out any longer.

We ran screaming madly away

and left all our stuff to the insects

and rain that had ruined our day.

So next time we'll go to the movies,

or maybe just go to the mall.

That last time we went on a picnic

was really no picnic at all.

Ken Nesbitt

Tulips

- Read poems and comment on words and sounds, rhyme and rhythm. (2Rw3)
- Find factual information from different formats, e.g. charts, labelled diagrams. (2Rx4)
- Show some awareness that texts have different purposes. (2Rv1)

Resources

Photocopiable page 63; camera.

Starter

- Display an enlarged version of photocopiable page 65 and read the poem. Explain that roundabouts like these are common in the UK and no-one would walk through the traffic to try to stand on them because it is too dangerous.
- Now ask the learners to read it with you.
- Help them to clap out the beat – they will see that this is difficult because there is very little rhythm or rhyme in the poem.

Main activities

- Ask the learners to think about what pictures they could **see** in their minds from this poem. Would they be able to draw this roundabout with roads going to different places?
- Now ask them what they could **hear** if they were standing on the roundabout.
- Ask the learners to work with a partner to create a list of facts from the poem, for example which traffic went past and what noise did it make?
- Ask: *Do you think that the poet might have seen tulips on a roundabout and thought these were beautiful? What do you think the purpose of the poem is?* (Perhaps to tell people to notice beautiful flowers, even when they are in a hurry?)
- Ask: *Why are flowers planted on roundabouts?* (To brighten up the place, to help drivers feel cheerful, perhaps.)

- Go on a walk near the school or in the local park with the class and take photographs of any flowers planted nearby. Back at school, display the photographs large enough for all the learners to see. Ask them to choose one of the locations to write a poem about in the style of 'Tulips on the roundabout'. Remind them that they don't need to worry too much about rhythm or rhyme.

Plenary

- Divide the learners into small groups and ask them to say whether the following statements are true or false:
  - Flowers are planted on roundabouts.
  - Flowers help to make the world look beautiful.
  - It's silly to plant flowers on roundabouts.
  - The purpose of this poem is to say that tulips are beautiful.
  - The purpose of this poem is to tell people to notice beautiful things in the world.
- Come back together as a class and share the learners' thoughts.

Success criteria

Ask the learners:

- How does the poet help you see and hear things in this poem?
- Why does no-one touch the tulips?
- What do you think the poet is saying in this poem?

Ideas for differentiation

Support: Provide these learners with copies of the photographs from the walk. Ask them to choose one and stick it in the centre of a piece of paper and write words to describe what they saw and heard in the location around the photograph.

Extension: Ask these learners to use a thesaurus to find an interesting range of adjectives in their poem.

Tulips on the roundabout

The tulips stand where nobody goes

On the roundabout between the roads,

Some with yellow turbans on their heads

And some with red.

One road goes to the works

And one to school,

One under the railway bridge

And one to the swimming pool.

Peeping and screeching, the cars go past

The tulips in their turbans on the grass.

They never seem to notice

The lorries rumbling round

But stand quite still

On their special piece of ground,

As if they had flown through the air

On a green magic carpet

And landed there.

Stanley Cooke

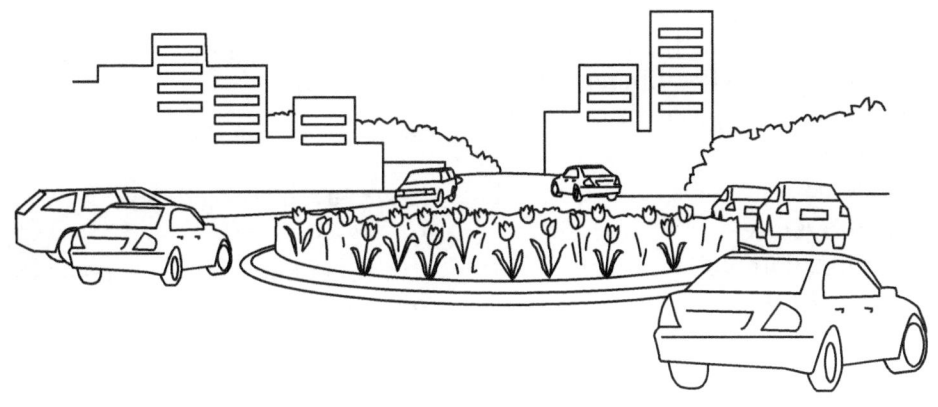

Unit assessment

Questions to ask

- Here are the first lines of some of the poems you have learnt – can you give me the next line? 'Puddle, splash, puddle, splash', 'One, two, off with that shoe!', 'We brought a rug for sitting on'.
- What is funny and what is sad about 'Jam on Toast' by Gareth Owen and 'One tongue' by Julia Donaldson?

- What is the special word we use to describe the beat of the poem?
- Explain how you used your voice to show how the speakers were feeling in the two bedtime poems.
- Why did you like one poem more than any of the others?
- Why were beautiful tulips planted on a busy roundabout?

Summative assessment activities

Observe the learners while they play these games. You will quickly be able to identify those who appear to be confident and those who may need additional support.

Playtime rhyme

This activity asks the learners to talk about the way two-syllable words can create pictures of a loud and noisy playtime.

You will need:

Photocopiable page 67, photocopied onto card and cut up into word cards.

What to do

- Hand out a card to each learner.
- Ask the learners to read their card and act out the word for the other learners to guess.
- Ask the learners to walk around the classroom and join together with words that are similar.
- Together, create a poem by arranging the cards to form a poem, putting the words together where the learners are in groups. Talk about the effects of having different or the same length lines, or of putting words that alliterate together.
- An example could be:

Playtime
running, skipping,
laughing
shouting, crying, wailing,
leaping, marching
PLAYTIME!

Syllable game

This game helps the learners to consolidate their knowledge of syllables in words, which helps them understand beat and rhythm in poems.

You will need:

Name cards for all the learners.

What to do

- Sit the learners in a circle and give each learner their name card.
- Call out a learner's name, for example 'Angelo'.
- Clap out the syllables An / ge / lo.
- Ask Angelo to copy and clap out the three syllables.
- Carry on until all the learners have done this.
- Ask them to arrange themselves into sets of 1, 2, 3, 4 and 5 syllable names.
- Call out the numbers in turn and tell the learners with that number of syllables in their name to stand up. Ask them all to say their names at the same time and clap the syllable(s).

Written assessment

Hand out photocopiable page 67 to each learner and ask them to use the words to write their own playtime poem.

Name: _____

Playtime words

walking	running	hopping	skipping	jumping
clapping	shouting	laughing	screaming	wheeling
turning	crying	wailing	crawling	climbing
hurrying	leaping	marching	pushing	pulling
shoving	stopping	starting	sighing	sobbing
sniffing	yowling	whining	yelling	weeping

Playtime poem

Write your own playtime poem. You could use some of the words listed above or choose your own. It can be a happy or sad playtime.

_____

_____

_____

_____

_____

_____

_____

Unit 2A: Traditional tales and stories from other cultures

Little Inchkin

Learning objectives

- Identify and describe story settings and characters, recognising that these may be from different times and places. (2Ri2)
- Talk about what happens at the beginning, in the middle or at the end of a story. (2Rw2)
- Begin to read with fluency and expression, taking some notice of punctuation, including speech marks. (2R07)

Resources

Internet access; *Little Inchkin* by Fiona French (Frances Lincoln) or a version of 'Issun-Boshi' a globe; pictures of lotus flowers and Japanese temples.

Starter

- Introduce *Little Inchkin* by Fiona French. (If you do not have a copy of the book you can use another version of the story known as 'Issun-Boshi' in Japan; adapt the activities accordingly.) Explain that the story starts with a visit to a temple by Hana, a Japanese wife, and Tanjo, her husband.
- Show pictures of lotus flowers and watch a film of someone walking around a Japanese temple (for example the first few minutes of www.youtube.com/watch?v=zwONZ-kHKSE&feature=related). Listen to the sound of Japanese temple bells. Locate Japan on the globe.

Main activities

- Open *Little Inchkin* at the first double-page spread showing Hana and Tanjo kneeling to Buddha with their gifts on the floor, and read this page to the learners.
- Select different learners to read the text with fluency and expression, using two different voices for Hana and Buddha.
- Turn to the next spread and ask different learners to read this page, modelling how to use your voice to show Hana's disappointment at the baby being so small – as small as a lotus flower.

- Show the end pages of the book that are covered in lotus flowers. Measure the little figure and tell them that he was about 2 inches long (5cm). Tell the class that an 'inch' was a way of measuring in the past. Draw a line two inches long and say that he was named Little Inchkin, after this measure.
- Display the next spread ending with 'Maybe I will find a way to grow as tall as other people'. Ask the class to read this silently, and then ask selected learners to read this again fluently and with expression.
- Hand out photocopiable page 69 for the learners to complete in pairs.

Plenary

- Play 'Thumbs up, thumbs down': Make statements that the learners can agree with or disagree with by showing a 'thumbs up' or 'thumbs down' signal, for example: *Japan is a flat country. Hana and Tanjo were married. There are many temples in Japan.* Choose different learners to say why they agree or disagree with each statement.

Success criteria

Ask the learners:

- Where is this story set?
- Did this story happen now, or a long time ago?
- Who are the main characters?
- How do you know when people are talking?

Ideas for differentiation

Support: Write correct answers for the first three questions on photocopiable page 69 on three separate strips and give them to these learners. Ask them to decide which answer matches which question and write these on the photocopiable page.

Extension: Ask these learners to find a variety of pictures of Japanese temples and draw them on their photocopiable page.

Name: _____

Little Inchkin

1. Answer the following questions about **Little Inchkin** by Fiona French.

   a) Where is the setting for this story?

   _____

   b) Is the story happening now, or a long time ago?

   _____

   c) Why were Hana, Tanjo and Inchkin unhappy?

   _____

   _____

   d) Draw a picture of Inchkin – show him as his exact size.

2. Draw pictures of Japanese temples, mountains and lotus flowers.

The main events

Learning objectives

- Talk about what happens at the beginning, in the middle or at the end of a story. (2Rw2)
- Discuss the meaning of unfamiliar words encountered in reading. (2R10)
- Extend experiences and ideas through role-play. (2SL9)

Resources

Photocopiable page 71; *Little Inchkin* by Fiona French (Frances Lincoln) or a version of the Japanese tale 'Issun-Boshi'; a series of questions and answers about the story on separate strips of paper.

Starter

- Ask the learners to talk about what has happened so far in the story.
- Explain these expressions before you read the middle section of the story: 'a suit of armour', 'swift-flowing tide', 'a special task', 'demons', 'lunged'.
- Continue reading the story up to 'The demon howled with pain and both the evil spirits fled away.' If you don't have a copy of the book, use a version of the tale readily available on the internet under its original name of 'Issun-Boshi'. Adapt the following activities to suit the version you find.

Main activities

- Ask the learners to talk about what has happened in the middle part of the story.
- Bring this story to life by asking the learners to create a series of dramatised scenes. Organise the class into groups and give each group one of the events from photocopiable page 71 to improvise as a scene. You will need to make sure that the groups have the right number of learners in them – between one and four depending on the scene. If necessary, have more than one group doing each scene.

- Give the learners time to discuss their scenes and who is going to say what. Tell them to improvise their scenes when they hear you say 'Action'.
- Ask the groups to tell the middle part of the story but to perform their scenes in order (going through twice if you have more than eight groups).
- Ask the learners to say what they enjoyed about the acting. Encourage them to give specific examples.
- Hand out photocopiable page 71 for the learners to complete.

Plenary

- Hand out the question-and-answer strips to pairs of learners. Ask them to move around the room, reading each other's strips until they find the answer to their question or the question for their answer.

Success criteria

Ask the learners:

- How does the middle part of the story start?
- How did Inchkin learn to be a skilled swordsman?
- What new words have you learnt in this story?
- How can improvising scenes help you remember the events?

Ideas for differentiation

Support: Place these learners in the larger groups for the improvisation, or ask them to share a part between them.

Extension: Ask these learners to take on the scenes where Inchkin is on his own, challenging them to create drama with them.

Sorting Inchkin

1. Cut out these events from the story of **Little Inchkin** and stick them in the right order on another piece of paper.

2. Draw a picture for each event.

The demons ran away.	He was lifted out of the river into a large boat.
Prince Sanjo told him he had to show him what a good swordsman he was.	Inchkin stabbed the demons with his sharp swords.
Inchkin made himself a suit of armour and became a skilled swordsman.	Inchkin had to sit with the princess in her carriage and guard her.
He sailed on the big river in a nutshell.	Two demons stopped the carriage moving forward.

Writing interesting sentences

Learning objectives

- Predict story endings. (2Ri1)
- Choose interesting words and phrases, e.g. in describing people and places. (2Wa2)
- Attempt to express ideas precisely, using a growing vocabulary. (2SL6)

Resources

Photocopiable page 73; *Little Inchkin* by Fiona French (Frances Lincoln) or a version of 'Issun-Boshi'; a range of photographs of nature; a pile of adjective cards that could describe the photographs you have.

Starter

- Ask the learners to recap on the main events in the middle part of the story *Little Inchkin* or 'Issun-Boshi'.
- Ask: *How do you predict the story will end?* Read aloud the options below one at a time and ask the learners to discuss the likelihood of each one in turn being the ending:
  - The two evil demons come back with two more demons and Inchkin runs away.
  - Inchkin decides to leave the princess and look for more adventures in different places in Japan.
  - Inchkin suddenly grows tall, the princess falls in love with him and they get married.
- Ask the learners to couch their responses as follows: *We think that this is unlikely to be the ending because …* or *We think that this is the most likely ending because …*
- Read the ending of the story together with the learners so that they can see whether they were right or not.

Main activities

- Draw a large picture of Inchkin on the board and ask the learners to think of some adjectives to describe him. Write the words they suggest around your drawing, expanding their thoughts when they get stuck, for example: 'brave', 'daring', 'fierce', 'confident', 'lion-hearted', 'fearless', 'unafraid'.

- Hand out photocopiable page 73 for the learners to complete. Make sure they understand all the vocabulary.
- Start a display of interesting words and phrases that can be used for all three books in this unit (*Little Inchkin* by Fiona French, *Rainbow Bird* by Eric Maddern and *Jamil's Clever Cat* by Fiona French [all Frances Lincoln]). Pin up a poster-sized piece of paper on the wall and head it 'Amazing words! Fantastic words!' Encourage the learners to suggest words and phrases that can be added to it across this unit.

Plenary

- Display a range of photographs of nature, for example a sunset, the moon, a rainbow, lightening, a hurricane, and so on. Give one of the adjectives cards to each learner and go round the room asking the learners to use their adjective to describe something in one of the photographs, for example 'a beautiful sunset', 'a silvery moon'.

Success criteria

Ask the learners:

- How did the story actually end?
- Was this ending like those in fairy stories such as 'Cinderella' and 'Sleeping Beauty'?
- Which words might describe kind characters?
- Why is the phrase 'as brave as a lion' a good one to use about Inchkin?

Ideas for differentiation

Support: Practise the Plenary activity beforehand with these learners so that they can contribute equally at this session.

Extension: Engineer for these learners to have adjectives that are more complex to use.

Name: _____

Writing interesting sentences

1. Choose two words from each box to make an interesting sentence.

a)

| cool | quiet | still | peaceful | restful |

The temple was _____ and _____.

b)

| gigantic | peaceful | tall | stunning | towering | majestic | flat |

The mountains were _____ and _____.

c)

| worried | anxious | fearful | afraid | concerned |

Hana was _____ and _____.

2. Choose one of the phrases from each box to finish the sentence.

a)

| as brave as a lion | as quick as a fox |

Inchkin was _____.

b)

| as beautiful as the setting sun | as beautiful as a rainbow |

The princess was _____.

3. Draw a picture on the back of this page to illustrate one of the sentences.

Rainbow Bird

Learning objectives

- Talk about what happens at the beginning, in the middle or at the end of a story. (2Rw2)
- Vary talk and expression to gain and hold the listener's attention. (2SL4)
- Comment on some vocabulary choices, e.g. adjectives. (2Rw1)

Resources

Photocopiable page 75; *Rainbow Bird* by Eric Maddern (Frances Lincoln) or a version of 'Rainbow Bird' from the internet; a globe; pictures of Australia including Aboriginal people and crocodiles.

Starter

- Tell the learners that the next story you will share with them, *Rainbow Bird* by Eric Maddern, is from Australia. If you don't have a copy of the book, use a version of 'Rainbow Bird' from the internet and adapt the lessons accordingly.
- Locate Australia on a globe and talk about where it is in relation to the school. Ask the learners if anyone has visited Australia, and if so what they remember about it. Show a range of photographs of Australia including pictures of deserts, beaches, kangaroos, crocodiles and Aboriginal people.
- Tell the learners that this story came from the Aboriginal people who have lived in Australia for thousands of years. Explain that this is a very old story that was originally told rather than written down.

Main activities

- Introduce the book but avoid showing the cover. Show the end pages of kangaroos hopping through some shady trees, with a desert in the background.
- Read the beginning of the story up to where Bird Woman 'flew back into the tree'. Give the learners time to talk about the beginning of the story.

- Draw their attention to the powerful adjectives used in the book so far by re-reading the first page and asking the learners to close their eyes and listen out for words that describe the Crocodile Man: 'rough', 'tough'; 'huge' and 'mean and scary'. Write these words on your 'Amazing Words! Fantastic Words!' list.
- Re-read the second page, pausing dramatically after the words 'Fire! Fire was his alone. Fire was his. Alone.' Ask the learners now to read it again with you in the same way. Move to the fifth spread and read it aloud, asking the learners to spot the powerful verbs used to describe the way the characters were talking: 'pleaded', 'snapped', 'croaked', 'sighed'. Add these to the list and talk about their meaning.
- Hand out individual copies of photocopiable page 75 for the learners to complete.

Plenary

- Ask the learners to sit in pairs with their completed photocopiable pages. Ask them to practise reading these with expression, noticing the speech marks.

Success criteria

Ask the learners:

- How did the story begin?
- When reading, how do you know when someone is speaking?
- Which words in this book are powerful adjectives and verbs?

Ideas for differentiation

Support: Ask these learners to draw a picture of a crocodile and write some labels, for example 'tough', 'skin', 'sharp', 'teeth', 'long tail', 'big eyes'.

Extension: Ask these learners to find the word 'say' in a children's thesaurus, make a list of other words for 'say' and write two sentences using two different verbs, for example 'shouted' and 'mumbled'.

Name: _____

Powerful words and phrases

1. Choose powerful adjectives from the box to complete the sentences.

Adjectives

rough   tough   huge   mean   scary

a) Crocodiles and alligators have skin that is _____

   and _____.

b) They are _____ creatures!

2. Choose powerful verbs to complete the sentences.

Verbs

begged   growled   pleaded   snapped   croaked   sighed

a) "Please give me some food," _____ Alfie.

b) "The princess is so beautiful," _____ Jack the toad.

c) "I wish I had something to wear to the ball," _____
   Cinderella.

3. Use these phrases to complete the sentences.

Phrases

huge and mean and scary   snarling and snapping

a) I could hear the beast _____ in the forest.

b) Out of the darkness came the bear. He was _____

   _____.

Different parts of a story

Learning objectives

● Talk about what happens at the beginning, in the middle or at the end of a story. (2Rw2)

● Vary talk and expression to gain and hold the listener's attention. (2SL4)

● Use the language of time, e.g. *suddenly, after that.* (2Wt2)

Resources

Photocopiable page 77; *Rainbow Bird* by Eric Maddern (Frances Lincoln) or a version of 'Rainbow Bird' from the internet; internet access.

Starter

• Read the middle and the end of *Rainbow Bird* by Eric Maddern or from a version of 'Rainbow Bird' from the internet.

• Ask the learners to discuss in pairs what they liked best about this part of the story.

• Show images of real rainbow birds from the internet and watch a film clip of aboriginal people making a fire with dry sticks (for example at www.youtube.com/watch?v= Jbyd0LuVoZw). Tell the learners that this story is the Aboriginal people's way of explaining how man found fire.

Main activities

• Draw the learners' attention to the way the story uses the language of time by showing these headings: 'Long ago', 'Time passed' and 'From that day on'. Talk about these headings in relation to the beginning, middle and end of *Rainbow Bird*.

• Hand out individual copies of photocopiable page 77. Divide the learners into three groups and ask each group to practise telling one of the sections of the story.

• Explain that the groups can decide how they retell their section: just taking it in turns to speak, or with some of the learners miming or acting as well, and so on. Explain that the notes on the page are just a reminder of the plot – tell them to use their own words to retell the story.

• Move around the groups as they rehearse. Model how they can vary talk and expression to gain and hold the attention of those listening, for example: 'He would **not** share it. Bird Woman **watched** and **waited**, **waited** and **watched** Crocodile Man'.

• When the groups are confident with their retelling and have rehearsed it, give each group some percussion instruments to add sound effects to their retelling.

Plenary

• Copy out short pieces of speech, either from this or another story, onto strips of paper. Ask volunteers to read them out, speaking as expressively as possible.

Success criteria

Ask the learners:

● What did Bird Woman ask Crocodile Man for in the middle of the story?

● Can you talk like the Bird Woman who sighed: "You're so mean"?

● Why do stories like this use phrases like 'Long ago', 'Time passed' and 'From that day on'?

Ideas for differentiation

Support: Make sure that these learners are part of a mixed-ability group so that they can take a full part in the story-telling activity.

Extension: Ask these learners to discuss whether Rainbow Bird should have stolen the fire-sticks – isn't stealing always wrong?

Talking about time

Use this plot summary for **Rainbow Bird** by Eric Maddern to retell the story in your own words and style.

Long ago

Crocodile Man kept the fire.

He was the Boss for fire.

He would not share it.

Bird Woman begged him for fire so that people could cook their food.

He took no notice.

Time passed

Bird woman waited and watched Crocodile Man.

He was very sleepy.

He yawned so much that Bird Woman snatched the fire sticks.

She flew everywhere giving fire to the trees to dry them so that these could be burned.

From that day on

People had fire for cooking, keeping warm, seeing in the dark.

The firesticks changed Bird Woman's feathers into rainbow colours.

She became Rainbow Bird.

Crocodile Man had to stay in the river.

Rainbow Bird could fly anywhere.

Word pictures

Learning objectives

● Comment on some vocabulary choices, e.g. adjectives. (2Rw1)

● Choose interesting words and phrases, e.g. in describing people and places. (2Wa2)

● Build and use collections of interesting and significant words. (2Wa3)

Resources

Photocopiable page 79; *Rainbow Bird* by Eric Maddern (Frances Lincoln) or a version of 'Rainbow Bird' from the internet; picture of a rainbow; internet access.

Starter

• Tell the learners that they are going to learn all about adjectives in this lesson, starting with colours, which are all adjectives because these describe the colour of something.

• Share the beautiful image of the Rainbow Bird on the tenth spread of *Rainbow Bird* by Eric Maddern or look again at pictures of rainbow birds on the internet. Discuss the colours of the birds' feathers and compare them to photographs of rainbows. Listen to and sing along to a version of the song 'I can sing a rainbow' (for example at www.youtube.com/watch?v=2kfoIABGpkY).

Main activities

• Tell the learners that colour adjectives help us to imagine the object more clearly, making writing more interesting for people to read.

• Model this by writing some up on the board: a red apple, a green handbag, a yellow pineapple – can the learners picture these in their heads? Could they draw a picture of these things?

• Move on to adjectives that could describe how these things would feel if you touched them, for example a smooth red apple, a soft green handbag, a spiky yellow pineapple.

• Hand out individual copies of photocopiable page 79 for the learners to complete.

• When they've finished, ask the learners to share their descriptions of their creature with a partner. Choose some that are interesting and read these out for the other learners to say why they enjoyed the description.

• Now ask the learners to write what the strange creature could see when it looked at them. Ask them to use adjectives to describe their own face and head. Model the beginning of this for them, for example: 'I was lying on the ground when a large creature picked me up and looked at me. I could see a pair of blue eyes and in the middle of his face there were two small black holes …'

• Create a subheading 'Awesome adjectives' on your 'Amazing words! Fantastic words!' chart and add the best adjectives used in the lesson.

Plenary

• Play a shopping memory game with the learners. Sit in a circle and say: *I went to the shops and bought a juicy red apple.* The next learner must then repeat what you said and then add another fruit, describing it with two adjectives, for example a yummy yellow banana, some sweet pink grapes, a hard green mango, and so on. Carry on round the circle adding items to the list until everyone has had a go remembering and adding to the list.

Success criteria

Ask the learners:

● What is the purpose of adjectives?

● Why are colours adjectives?

● Which adjectives might describe a toad?

● Why do writers use adjectives?

Ideas for differentiation

Support: Provide these learners with a set of black and white picture cards and ask them to pick one card at a time from the middle of the table and describe it by adding an adjective, for example a stripy cat, a tall giraffe, and so on.

Extension: Ask these learners to use a thesaurus and find different words for 'bright' and then make up some interesting sentences.

Name: _____

Awesome adjectives

1. Imagine that you have found a strange creature outside – it might be an alien from a different planet, something from the heart of the Amazon or a monster from a storybook! What does it look, feel and smell like? Describe your creature using adjectives from the list below, or use your own adjectives if you wish.

The way things look	The way things feel	The way things smell
grey	smooth	sweet
black	rough	fragrant
brown	slippery	smelly
greenish	wet	yucky
tall	slimy	nasty
short	lumpy	stinky
tiny	spiky	lemony

   a) I saw something moving on the ground. I looked more closely

and saw _____

_____

_____

   b) I touched it and it felt _____

_____

_____

   c) It smelled _____

_____

_____

2. Now draw a picture of your creature on the back of this page and label it with your adjectives.

Jamil's Clever Cat

Learning objectives

- Identify and describe story settings and characters, recognising that they may be from different times and places. (2Ri2)
- Extend experiences and ideas through role-play. (2SL9)
- Write in clear sentences using capital letters, full stops and question marks. (2Wp1)

Resources

A globe; internet access; *Jamil's Clever Cat* by Fiona French (Frances Lincoln); a sari; photocopiable page 81.

Starter

- Ask the learners if anyone has visited India or Bengal and encourage them to talk about their experiences. Locate both places on a globe. Show some pictures and play some music from Bengal (for example at www.youtube.com/watch?v=Yr1xmJHNq5s and www.shunya.net/Pictures/NorthIndia/WestBengal.htm).
- Introduce the story of *Jamil's Clever Cat* and tell the learners that this story is similar to the story of 'Puss in Boots'.
- Explain that Jamil is a weaver and show some pictures of weaving.

Main activities

- Display the cover of the book, asking the learners to look at the lovely material of the sari – suggest that perhaps Jamil wove it. If possible, show the learners a real sari.
- Read the first double-page spread, which tells the reader that Jamil lives on the 'poor side of town', and that his cat, Sardul, weaves the beautiful fabric while Jamil makes the material into tunics and saris.

- Read the second double-page spread together with the learners. Try to capture the unhappiness of Jamil and the optimism of Sardul by the way you read this spread. Discuss the idiom 'work our fingers to the bone' with the learners. Divide the class into two, one half reading Jamil's words in an unhappy manner, the other half reading Sardul's words in an upbeat, positive manner. Ask them to pair up with a partner from the other half of the class and role-play a conversation between Jamil and his cat.
- Move on to read the third double-page spread and discuss the story so far.
- Hand out individual copies of photocopiable page 81 and ask the learners to complete the task. Tell them you expect them to write sentences that are easy to understand, and that they must remember capital letters, full stops and question marks correctly.

Plenary

- Draw a picture of Jamil and Sardul and ask the learners to share with you what they have learnt so far about these characters. Make a list under each picture.
- Hot-seat first Jamil, and then Sardul, and get the learners to ask you the questions they have prepared on photocopiable page 81.

Success criteria

Ask the learners:

- Where is this story set?
- Who are the main characters?
- What did you learn about Jamil and Sardul during 'hot-seating'?
- Why is it really important to write sentences with all the correct punctuation?

Ideas for differentiation

Support: Ask these learners to talk to an adult helper about what they have learnt about Jamil and Sardul first so they can write more confidently.

Extension: Ask these learners to think of a different way that Jamil might get rich – without marrying a princess.

Name: _____

What I know about Jamil and Sardul

1. Write what you know about Jamil so far in the box below.
    What else would you like to know? Write a question to ask him.

What I know about Jamil:

_____

_____

_____

My question for Jamil:

_____

_____

2. Write what you know about Sardul so far in the box below.
    What else would you like to know? Write a question to ask him.

What I know about Sardul:

_____

_____

_____

My question for Sardul:

_____

_____

Wedding plans

Learning objectives

- Discuss the meaning of unfamiliar words encountered in reading. (2R10)
- Begin to read with fluency and expression, taking some notice of punctuation, including speech marks. (2R07)
- Vary talk and expression to gain and hold the listener's attention. (2SL4)

Resources

Jamil's Clever Cat by Fiona French (Frances Lincoln); internet access; photocopiable page 83.

Starter

- Ask the learners to talk about what has happened in the story of *Jamil's Clever Cat* so far – and if they have any idea of what Sardul's plan might be.
- Before reading the next set of spreads, ensure that the learners know the meaning of: 'sauntered', 'a small token of his esteem', 'flattered', 'a chorus of creatures'.
- Now read the next five spreads up to 'So Jamil and his cat went into the palace alone.'

Main activities

- Read the next spread, where Sardul saunters into the garden and offers the sari to the princess, saying that it is a 'token of esteem' from his master. Ask the learners to read this again showing you they can really express how flattered the princess is and how well Sardul tells lies about his master.
- Do the same for the next spread where Sardul secures an offer of marriage for his master. As they make their wedding clothes they decide to invite wedding guests – read the next spread and ask the learners in pairs to discuss why Sardul decides to invite animals to the wedding, rather than people.

- Move on to the next spread where all is revealed: the animals gathering in the palace gardens sound like a thousand people talking; the Rajah decides that it would be very expensive to invite them all to the wedding, so they just invite Jamil and Sardul – which was Sardul's plan!
- Read the description of the chorus of animals: 'a roaring of tigers, a chattering of monkeys, a trumpeting of elephants'. Listen to a parakeet talking to get a sense of the noise just one of these animals might make (for example at www.youtube.com/watch?v=5b2p9e059SA).
- Hand out individual copies of photocopiable page 83 for the learners to complete.

Plenary

- Write out a number of things the characters say on separate strips of paper. Hand them out to pairs of learners and ask them to discuss who said the words on their strip of paper and why, then invite the learners to read their sentence to the class, fluently and with expression.

Success criteria

Ask the learners:

- Explain what these words mean: 'weaver', 'waistcoat', 'sari', 'a token of esteem'.
- Why is it important to read aloud without making any mistakes?
- Which punctuation marks tell you that someone is speaking?
- How do listeners feel when they are listening to stories that are read well and with expression?

Ideas for differentiation

Support: Ask these learners to design a pattern for a sari.

Extension: Ask these learners to think of some more words to describe Sardul that mean 'clever'. They can use a thesaurus to help them.

Name: _____

Animal noises

1. Read the sounds made by each of the animals below:

maaaah

ha, ha, ha, ha

grrrrrr

bu-hoo, bu-hoo

'Where did he go?'

2. In the story there was a 'roaring of tigers and a chattering of monkeys'. Write similar descriptions for the animals above. The first one has been done for you.

    a) A bleating of goats.

    b) A _____ of hyenas.

    c) A _____ of buffaloes.

    d) A _____ of Bengal eagle owls.

    e) A _____ of parakeets.

Thinking about character

Learning objectives

- Make simple inferences from the words on the page, e.g. about feelings. (2Ri3)
- Extend experiences and ideas through role-play. (2SL9)
- Write in clear sentences using capital letters, full stops and question marks. (2Wp1)

Resources

Internet access; *Jamil's Clever Cat* by Fiona French (Frances Lincoln); photocopiable page 85; strips of paper.

Starter

- Ask the learners to recap on the story so far. Check that the learners understand the words 'loom' and 'confessed' ready for the remaining pages.
- Show a film clip of someone weaving on a hand loom in India (for example at www.youtube.com/watch?v=V0njHAkTpnQ&feature=related).
- Finish reading *Jamil's Clever Cat* to the learners.

Main activities

- Place the learners in mixed-ability pairs to discuss the following questions. Ask them to role-play each small scene as they go along, to capture their thoughts about the characters.
  - *Why was Jamil thinking about his loom during his wedding feast?*
  - *Why wasn't Jamil thinking about ruling the country after his marriage?*
  - *Which two things shocked the princess when she moved into Jamil's home?*
  - *Why didn't she leave and go back to the palace?*
  - *Who do you think taught the princess how to weave?*
  - *How did they become rich?*
  - *How did Jamil and his wife show that they were so very happy when the Rajah and Ranee visited them?*
- Share the thoughts of the learners, sensitively discussing any differences of opinion.

- Explain the role of an author and illustrator in a book and explain that Fiona French works as both. Look again at *Little Inchkin* (the book itself or images of it on the internet). Point out that in *Jamil's Clever Cat*, she worked with another artist, Dick Newby, who created the beautiful paper Fiona French used in her illustrations.
- Hand out individual copies of photocopiable page 85 and ask the learners to complete the task in pairs, checking that their questions are clearly written and correctly punctuated.

Plenary

- Prepare some statements on strips of paper that could be made by characters in *Jamil's Clever Cat*, for example 'I am not a happy man' or 'I love my master'. Make multiple copies of each statement and hand two or three to each pair of learners. Ask them to discuss who might have made these statements. Hand out blank bits of paper and ask the learners to write statements for another pair to guess.

Success criteria

Ask the learners:

- What does the verb 'sighed' tell you about Jamil?
- What does the word 'flattered' tell you about the princess?
- What can you learn from role-play?
- What does a question mark tell you at the end of a sentence?

Ideas for differentiation

Support: Make sure that each of these learners is placed with a learner who can write down the questions they think of together.

Extension: Ask these learners to write what they think about Sardul saying: 'Did I not tell you the truth?' and 'My master is the richest man in the world!'

Name: _____

Fiona French

Here is some information about the author Fiona French:

Fiona studied art at college in England. Then she started drawing pictures for children's books. She won a prize for drawing brilliant pictures for a book called **Snow White in New York**. She was the writer and illustrator for **Little Inchkin**. She has illustrated lots more books.

Now think of some questions you could ask Fiona if she visited your class. The first two have been done for you.

Questions to ask Fiona French

1. Do you have the most amazing cat in all the world?

2. Have you been to Bengal?

3. _____

4. _____

5. _____

6. _____

7. _____

Story connectives

- Use the language of time, e.g. *suddenly, after that*. (2Wt2)
- Articulate clearly so that others can hear. (2SL3)
- Vary talk and expression to gain and hold the listener's attention. (2SL4)

Jamil's Clever Cat by Fiona French (Frances Lincoln); display of time connectives; photocopiable page 87.

Starter

- Tell the learners that they are going to learn to tell a simple version of *Jamil's Clever Cat*. Explain that this will help them with their story-writing in the next session.
- Display this very simple outline of the story and ask the class to re-read it together:
  - Jamil was a poor weaver.
  - Jamil wanted to marry the princess.
  - Sardul, his cat, took a sari and a waistcoat to the princess.
  - The princess showed the gifts to the Rajah.
  - The Rajah said Jamil could marry the princess.
  - Jamil and the princess were married.
  - Jamil took the princess to his house.
  - The princess learnt how to weave.
  - Jamil and the princess became rich.

Main activities

- Display an extensive list of story connectives including: 'Once upon a time', 'One day', 'One morning', 'Immediately', 'Next', 'Later', 'After', 'Soon after that', 'So', 'When', 'Because', 'Luckily', 'Fortunately', 'Unfortunately', 'Finally', 'Eventually', 'In the end' and 'At long last'.
- Model writing the opening of a new version of *Jamil's Clever Cat*, talking aloud about the decisions you are making. Model trying out different connectives: *We need to choose a connective to start off the story. We could choose 'Once upon a time' as this is a very old traditional story. How about: 'Once upon a time there was a poor weaver called Jamil'?*

- Hand out photocopiable page 87 to the learners in small groups and ask them to practise reading this aloud.
- Display an enlarged version of the story, and as a class learn to tell the story by heart. First read the story several times together, setting a slow pace and telling the learners to articulate the words clearly. Then, gradually hide more and more of the story until the learners know it by heart confidently. Model how to use your voice to add drama to the story.

Plenary

- Arrange the learners into small groups and ask them to retell 'Little Red Riding Hood' using time connectives from their chart. Ask them to tell the story going around the group and saying a sentence each.

Ask the learners:

- Can you think of some of the words the writer uses to start off the story?
- Why is it important to speak clearly when you are reading a story aloud?
- How can a reader use his voice to catch the interest of the listeners?

Support: Add pictures to photocopiable page 87 to act as extra prompts for these learners to retell this story successfully.

Extension: Ask these learners to learn to tell a version of 'Puss in Boots'.

Retelling Jamil's Clever Cat

Raise your hands and make a circle in the air to signal the story opening.

Once upon a time, there was a poor weaver called Jamil.

Jamil thought that if only he could marry the princess, he would be rich.

So Sardul, his cat, took a sari and a waistcoat to the princess.

Immediately, the princess showed the gifts to the Rajah.

Fortunately, the Rajah said Jamil could marry the princess.

Soon after that, Jamil and the princess were married.

Later, Jamil took the princess to his house.

Then, the princess learned how to weave.

Finally, Jamil and the princess became rich.

Fold your arms to signal the end of the story.

My own version

Learning objectives

- Use the structures of familiar poems and stories in developing own writing. (2W05)
- Structure a story with a beginning, middle and end. (2Wt1)
- Use the language of time, e.g. *suddenly*, *after that*. (2Wt2)
- Plan writing through discussion or by speaking aloud. (2W06)

Resources

Photocopiable page 89.

Starter

- Display an enlarged version of photocopiable page 89 and tell the learners that they must now add some more sentences to this simple version to make it a more interesting story.
- Model extending the opening, talking aloud about your choices, for example: *I'm going to add some dialogue here as a quick way to show character and get the story started: 'Once upon a time, there was a poor weaver called Jamil. "Oh, Sardul", said Jamil one day. "We will never be rich if we carry on like this. We need a plan."'* Talk about how you are punctuating the sentence.
- Say: *Now, how shall we extend the next sentence to make the story interesting?* Ask a pair of learners for a suggestion, for example: "I can help you with your plan, master," said clever Sardul. "Give me the two most gorgeous garments we have in the house."
- Help the next pair to extend the next sentence, perhaps: 'The sari was crimson with gold stripes at the edges; it sparkled in the sunlight. The waistcoat was every shade of purple and blue you could think of.'
- Carry on asking different pairs of learners for ideas to extend each sentence in turn. Each time, model how you would write their sentence, talking about punctuation and asking for extra adjectives or dialogue where appropriate.

Main activities

- Hand out photocopiable page 89 and ask all the learners to write their own extended version of the story, using some of the ideas from the lesson if they wish, for example discussing their ideas with a friend first. Remind them that they should use adjectives and interesting verbs and some dialogue to brighten up their writing.

Plenary

- Select several good-quality finished stories and ask the learners who wrote them to rehearse reading aloud what they have written.
- Gather the class together and ask them to listen to these three stories, responding after each reading with a positive statement, for example: 'I liked it when you said that Sardul was a liar!'

Success criteria

Ask the learners.

- Is it easier to write stories based on those you have already heard?
- Do all stories have a beginning, a middle and an ending?
- Would you enjoy a story that did not have an ending?
- Do time words like 'Once upon a time' or 'After that' help to move a story along from the beginning to the middle to the ending?
- Do you find it easier to write a story after talking about your ideas first?

Ideas for differentiation

Support: Provide these learners with a selection of ready-written sentences that they can read and add to photocopiable page 89.

Extension: Challenge these learners to write their version of the story without using the photocopiable page.

Name: _____

Jamil's Clever Cat

Write your own version of **Jamil's Clever Cat** by filling in more detail between the sentences provided:

Once upon a time, there was a poor weaver called Jamil.

_____

_____

Jamil thought that if only he could marry the princess he would be rich.

_____

_____

So Sardul, his cat, took a sari and a waistcoat to the princess.

_____

_____

Immediately, the princess showed the gifts to the Rajah. _____

_____

Fortunately, the Rajah said Jamil could marry the princess.

_____

_____

Soon after that, Jamil and the princess were married. _____

_____

Later, Jamil took the princess to his house. _____

_____

Then the princess learnt how to weave. _____

_____

Finally, Jamil and the princess became rich. _____

_____

Unit assessment

Questions to ask

- Can you remember where the three stories studied in this unit were set?
- Can you say what you learnt about Inchkin from *Little Inchkin* by Fiona French?
- What did you learn about Bird Woman from *Rainbow Bird* by Eric Maddern?
- What things did Sardul, from *Jamil's Clever Cat* by Fiona French, do that were so clever?
- Which character from these three stories did you find the most interesting?
- Can you explain why writers use adjectives in a story?

Summative assessment activities

Observe the learners while they play these games. You will quickly be able to identify those who appear to be confident and those who may need additional support.

Walk like the verb, Talk like the verb!

This game assesses the learners' understanding of the impact of different verbs in their writing.

You will need:

A set of verb cards for the following words: 'yell', 'whisper', 'shout', 'laugh', 'screech', 'point', 'stretch', 'creep', 'run', 'stroll', 'dawdle', 'skip'.

What to do

- Sit the learners in a circle and place the pile of verb cards in the middle. Ask the learners to take turns to take a verb card from the pile, read it secretly and then mime or act the verb.
- Can the other learners guess what the verb is?
- Ask the learners to discuss why all these verbs are better than just writing or saying 'said' and 'walked'.

Guess who?

This game assesses the learners' deduction skills.

You will need:

Separate strips of paper with the following sentences on them:

1. This lady did not love her baby boy.
2. This creature is mean and tough and scary.
3. This creature is cunning and clever and a very good friend to his master.
4. This creature has feathers that shine like a rainbow.
5. This man is a brave fighter and an excellent swordsman.
6. This creature is very patient and spends a long time watching and waiting.
7. These evil creatures are hot and fiery and dangerous.
8. This lady weaves the best saris in the world.
9. This man suddenly became very tall.

What to do

- Divide the learners into three teams and give each team a set of character descriptions.
- On 'Go" the learners must take turns to read the descriptions out loud, discuss who the character might be and write the name on the back of the slip.
- Give the first team to finish the task a bonus point.
- Read out all the descriptions and give the name of the character. Ask the teams to give themselves a point for each correct answer.

Written assessment

Hand out photocopiable page 91 for the learners to complete individually. This will help to assess their understanding of and ability to use interesting adjectives and verbs.

Name: _____

Making sentences interesting

1. Rewrite these sentences to make them more interesting.
   Use words from below or choose your own.
   The first one has been done for you.

> silvery   dark   quiet   old   battered
>
> ancient   tiny   trembling   fluttering

   a)   I saw the moon last night.
   I saw a silvery moon last night.

   b)   I walked through a wood last night.

   _____

   c)   I closed the door and went home.

   _____

   d)   I picked up the bird and put it back in its nest.

   _____

2. Change the verb <u>said</u> to show how the person is feeling.
   The first one has been done for you.

   a)   "Give me that!" he said.
   "Give me that!" he roared.

   b)   "Yes, please" she said.

   _____

   c)   "I am tired," she said.

   _____

   d)   "Go away!" she said.

   _____

Unit 2B: Explanations and dictionary entries

Why we come to school

- Attempt to express ideas precisely, using a growing vocabulary. (2SL6)
- Find factual information from different formats, e.g. charts, labelled diagrams. (2Rx4)
- Use mainly simple and compound sentences, with *and / but* to connect ideas. *Because* may begin to be used in a complex sentence. (2Wp3)

Resources

Large pieces of paper and pens; photocopiable page 93; robot or alien toy.

Starter

- Write up the heading: 'Why we come to school' on the board. Ask the learners to discuss the subject in small groups, writing down their ideas on a large piece of paper. Move around the groups, encouraging the learners to articulate their ideas clearly and precisely.
- Ask the groups to present their lists to the class and discuss the different ideas that the learners have come up with. Ask: *What was the most common idea? What was the most interesting?*

Main activities

- Hand out photocopiable page 93 to each group. Ask the learners to discuss the information on the page and add any new ideas to their list.
- Introduce the key features of an explanation: an introductory sentence, a series of points that explain the subject, a concluding sentence.
- Tell them that the connectives 'because' and 'so' are very useful when writing explanations because they introduce information that explains.
- Give an oral example of an explanation modelling: 'We come to school because we want to learn lots of things. We come to school to learn to read and write so that we can get a job. We learn to be kind and tolerant because at school we meet lots of different children ...', and so on.

- Ask the learners to work in pairs to write their own explanation of why they go to school, using three or four ideas from their group list.

Plenary

- With the whole class together, bring out a robot or an alien toy. Tell the learners that he has just landed on this planet and wants to know what school is for, because no-one goes to school on his planet!
- Ask the learners in turns to explain why they come to school, using sentences with 'because' and 'so' in them.
- In your best robot voice, question the learners about what they have told you.

Success criteria

Ask the learners:

- Why is it important to explain ideas very carefully?
- Can people get information from pictures, as well as from words?
- Can you remember a sentence about school that has the word 'because' in it?
- Why is the word 'because' so important in sentences?

Ideas for differentiation

Support: Give these learners a set of pictures of school activities to use as an oral text for an explanation.

Extension: Ask these learners to explain why it is important to study specific subjects such as literacy or PE.

Life at school

Discuss these activities that take place in school and add any new ideas to your list.

Music	Maths	Reading
	20 + 15 = 35	
Science	**Play time**	**PE**
Assembly	**Work in class**	**Working together**
A school might start off the day with an assembly. Children can listen to stories that teach them how to be kind and caring. They may also sing together.	Children can enjoy learning about lots of new things. They also learn to concentrate and work hard.	Children must learn how to get on well with each other and work in teams. They must take turns, speak clearly and help other children. They must also learn to follow school rules such as not running indoors.

Explain how to make a toy car move faster

Learning objectives

- Recount experiences and explore possibilities. (2SL1)
- Explain plans and ideas, extending them in the light of discussion. (2SL2)
- Use mainly simple and compound sentences, with *and* / *but* to connect ideas. *Because* may begin to be used in a complex sentence. (2Wp3)

Resources

A toy car; a long piece of wood for ramps; four bricks; photocopiable page 95.

Starter

- Tell the learners that they are going to investigate how to make a toy car go faster and then write an explanation for another learner.
- Put the ramp on the floor and place the car on it. Ask them why the car isn't moving. (It is on the flat, does not have a wind-up motor, is not battery operated, and so on.) Ask them to discuss how to get the car moving without pushing it. (Raise the ramp with something, for example bricks).
- Take two bricks and make a ramp. Tell the learners that it is a gentle slope, which means it is not very steep. Place the car on top of the ramp. Get the learners to say 'Ready, steady, go!' and let the car go. Ask them what happened (the car moved) and why (because it was on a slope).

Main activities

- Ask the learners: *How could we make the car go faster?* (Make the slope steeper.) Ask: *How could you do that?* (By adding two more bricks.) Get the learners to say 'Ready, steady, go!' and let the car go again.
- Ask: *Why did the car go faster?* (Because the slope was steeper.) Ask them for more detail about this. (Because it was steeper the wheels turned faster and the car moved more quickly.)

- Hand out photocopiable page 95 and ask the learners to label the pictures then write a simple explanation of why the car went faster. Ask them to use sentences that have the word 'because' in them.
- Use this experiment to start a class booklet called 'Our book of explanations'.

Plenary

- Write 'The car goes faster down the higher ramp' on the board. Ask the learners to choose which of the following clauses would be best to use to finish this sentence for an explanation text:
  - 'and reaches the bottom of the ramp more quickly.'
  - 'and its wheels go round faster too.'
  - 'because it's going down a steeper slope.'
- Agree that the final option would be best because of its use of the connective 'because'.

Success criteria

Ask the learners:

- Why did this experiment use two different heights of ramp?
- How did the pictures help you to write the explanation of what happened?
- Which connective is very useful when trying to explain something?

Ideas for differentiation

Support: Arrange for these learners to conduct this experiment themselves, and take photographs of both ramps, which they can display and label. Provide them with a completed explanation to say orally.

Extension: Ask these learners to write an explanation with the title: 'Why do books have pictures?', writing at least two sentences and using the connective 'because'.

Name: _____

How to make a toy car move faster

1. Label the diagrams using the words in the box below.

> car   gentle slope   steeper slope   ramp   two bricks   four bricks

2. Complete the sentences to explain what is happening.

How to make a toy car move faster

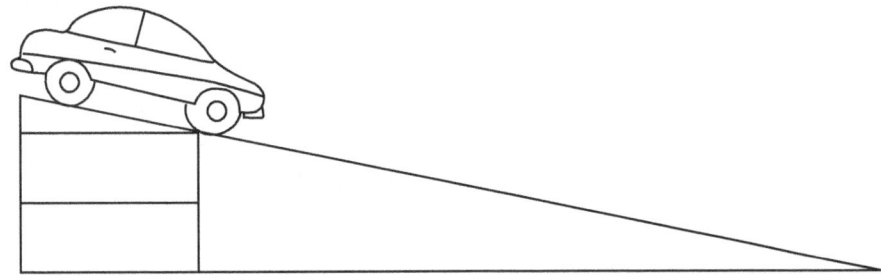

a) At first the car went down the gentle ramp quite slowly because

_____

_____

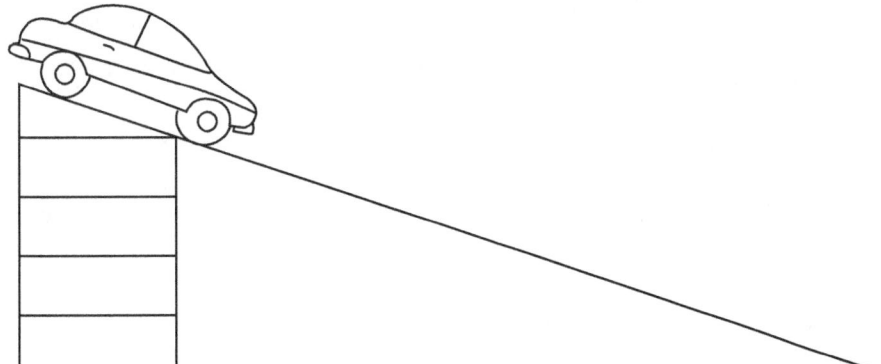

b) Then the car went down the steeper ramp faster because _____

_____

_____ and so the wheels

_____

How a tractor works

Learning objectives

- Find factual information from different formats, e.g. charts, labelled diagrams. (2Rx4)
- Discuss the meaning of unfamiliar words encountered in reading. (2R10)
- Use mainly simple and compound sentences, with *and / but* to connect ideas. *Because* may begin to be used in a complex sentence. (2Wp3)

Resources

A bicycle tyre; photocopiable page 97; internet access.

Starter

- Tell the learners that they are going to learn about how tractors work.
- Before handing out photocopiable page 97, explain the meanings of some of the labels: 'seed drill' – an implement fixed to the tractor for dropping seeds into the ground as the plough moves; 'bonnet' – the cover for the engine; 'deep tread' – show the bicycle tyre and say the tread on the big tyres is as deep as their fingers!; 'plough' – an implement fixed to the tractor for cutting and turning the soil ready for planting.
- Hand out photocopiable page 97 and ask the learners in pairs to read the labels and talk about the tractor diagrams together. Explain that the smaller wheels at the front help tractors to turn left or right easily.
- Watch a film clip of tractors ploughing (for example at www.youtube.com/watch?v=B43JyTSknl0&feature=related). Ask them what they see happening. (The plough fixed onto the tractor has heavy sharp blades that break up soil and cut furrows for planting. A furrow is a deep line cut in the soil for seeds.)

Main activities

- Ask the learners questions about the tractor to prepare them for completing photocopiable page 97:
  - *Why do you think it has a powerful engine?* (It is very heavy in itself; it pulls heavy machinery and does heavy work.)
  - *Tell me about the wheels. Why do you think the back wheels are huge and wide?* (To make it safe to drive on steep fields; to manoeuvre on bumpy ground.)
  - *How does the plough make deep furrows?* (The plough easily digs up the earth because it has very sharp blades that turn over. The blades are at an angle so they can cut through the earth and break it up.)
- Ask the learners to complete the sentences on photocopiable page 97.

Plenary

- Ask a learner to read out their explanation of how a tractor works.

Success criteria

Ask the learners:

- What information did you learn about tractors from pictures and the film?
- Can you explain what a seed drill and a bonnet are?
- What is 'tread' in a tyre?
- Can you think of a sentence with 'because' in it that gives a bit of information about a tractor?

Ideas for differentiation

Support: Provide these learners with ready-made sentences about tractors that they can re-order to create an explanation text.

Extension: Ask these learners to find out more information on how a seed drill works and write an extra sentence about it.

Name: _____

How a tractor works

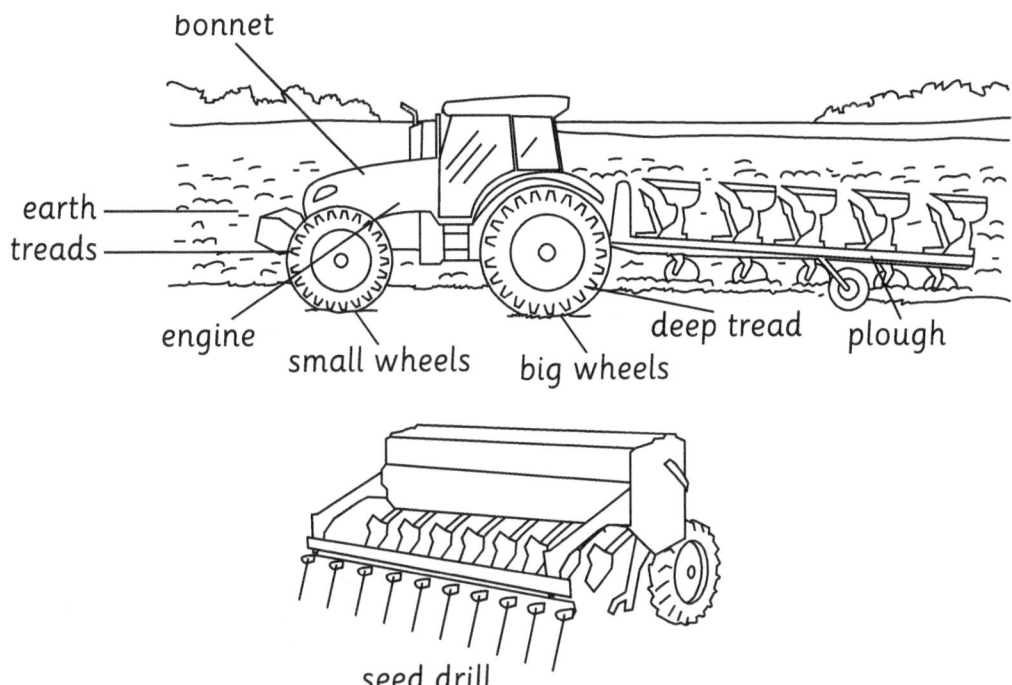

Finish the sentences below to explain how a tractor works.
The first one has been done for you.

1. A tractor has a powerful engine because it is a heavy machine to drive and it often pulls very heavy attachments.

2. The wheels of a tractor are huge and wide because _____

_____.

3. The treads on the tyres are deep because _____

_____.

4. The plough can be fixed on the _____

5. The tractor drags the plough over the _____

6. The plough easily digs up the earth because it has _____

_____.

7. It makes furrows for _____.

8. The farmer attaches the seed drill when _____

_____.

Reading flowcharts

Learning objectives

- Find factual information from different formats, e.g. charts, labelled diagrams. (2Rx4)
- Write in clear sentences using capital letters, full stops and question marks. (2Wp1)
- Use a variety of simple organisational devices in non-fiction, e.g. headings, captions. (2Wt4)

Resources

Photocopiable page 99.

Starter

- Display an enlarged version of the flowchart on photocopiable page 99 with the captions hidden. Ask the learners to describe what is happening from the beginning to the end of the flowchart.
- Reveal the captions and ask the learners to read these aloud.
- Ask if they found the flowchart an easy way to get information.

Main activities

- Write the following sentences on the board and ask the learners to use them to create their own flowchart for 'From seed to apple pie!'.
  - Save some apple seeds and let them dry out.
  - Cover your seeds with a damp paper towel and put them in the fridge for up to a month.
  - Plant the seedlings in a small pot of potting compost and water it every day.
  - When it is bigger, plant it in a bigger pot.
  - When it is 20 cm tall, plant it in the garden.
  - Water it every week.
  - Wait patiently for the apples to grow. (You will have grown up by then!)
  - Roll out some pastry in a pie tin and cover it with sliced apples and sugar.
  - Cover the apples with another layer of pastry. Cook in the oven.
  - Serve with custard or ice-cream.
  - Save any seeds to grow another apple tree.

- Ask the learners how many boxes they will need to draw for their flowchart. Then let them get started, copying the stages from the board or writing their own versions. Tell them to add an illustration for each stage.

Plenary

- Write the information from 'From seed to apple pie!' as one paragraph. Ask the learners which is easier to read and get information from: a paragraph or a flowchart?
- Write the sentences for the apple flowchart on strips of paper and hand them out to individual learners in a random order. Ask the learners to see how quickly they can organise themselves into a flowchart, linking hands to represent the flow of arrows.

Success criteria

Ask the learners:

- What are the arrows for in the flowchart?
- Why are flowcharts easy to get information from?
- Why is it harder to find the information you need from a paragraph of writing?
- What was the first information and picture in the 'From seed to apple pie!' flowchart?

Ideas for differentiation

Support: Provide a set of short captions for the 'From seed to apple pie!' flowchart that these learners can stick in the chart in the right order.

Extension: Ask these learners to draw a flowchart for 'From seed to pumpkin soup' or another recipe.

From seed to loaf

1.

Wheat seeds are planted in furrows using a seed drill.

Millions of seeds are planted.

2.

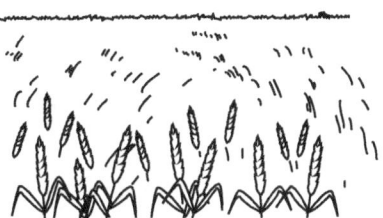

Rain and sun help to make the seeds grow into plants.

3.

The wheat is harvested and ground to make flour.

4.

The flour is mixed with water and yeast to make dough.
The risen dough is baked in the oven. The bread is ready.

The life cycle of a butterfly

Learning objectives

- Recount experiences and explore possibilities. (2SL1)
- Use simple non-fiction texts as a model for writing. (2W04)
- Use past and present tenses accurately (if not always consistently). (2Wp4)

Resources

Internet access; photocopiable page 101; music; a beanbag; a set of past-tense cards ('ate', 'drank', 'crawled', 'slept').

Starter

- Tell the learners that they are going to write an explanation of the life cycle of a butterfly.
- Watch a film clip of the life cycle of a butterfly (for example at www.youtube.com/watch?v=zxB-G2ItHGo&feature=related). Together, recap on the four stages of the life of a butterfly: egg, caterpillar, chrysalis and butterfly.

Main activities

- Using the time words 'First', 'Then', 'Next' and 'Finally', model orally how to say the stages aloud: *First, the butterfly lays an egg on a leaf.*
- Draw a blank version of the flowchart from photocopiable page 101 on the board. Tell the learners that the life cycle of all living things can be written in a circular flowchart.
- Ask the learners to help you write the life cycle of a butterfly: *We need a heading for this life cycle. Yes – 'The life cycle of a butterfly'. Tell me what to write in the first stage. 'First the butterfly lays an egg on a leaf.' Good – you have used the time word 'First'. Do you know why it lays it on a leaf?* (So that when the egg hatches into a caterpillar it can start eating immediately.) *Now tell me what happens afterwards: The egg hatches out. Yes. Which time word will I use now? 'Then the egg hatches out into a caterpillar.' Remember we use the present tense for explanations: hatches and not hatched.*

- Continue in this way to complete the flowchart.
- Wipe the board clean, hand out photocopiable page 101 and ask the learners to fill in the text for the flowchart.

Plenary

- Play 'Musical tenses'. Create a set of past-tense verb cards ('ate', 'drank', 'crawled', 'slept', 'flew', 'hopped', 'jumped', 'lay', 'stretched'). Ask the learners to get into a circle and place the cards in the middle. Give a beanbag to the first learner. Play some music and start passing the beanbag round the circle. When the music stops, the learner with the beanbag must run to the middle, take a card, read the word loudly and turn it into the present tense.

Success criteria

Ask the learners:

- Was it helpful to say this life cycle with a partner first, before writing it?
- Why did we write the life cycle of a butterfly in a flowchart?
- Which tense is used in this explanation?
- Which 'time' words were useful?

Ideas for differentiation

Support: Print some pictures from the internet of the four stages of the life cycle of a butterfly and ask these learners to stick them in the flowchart in the correct order.

Extension: Ask these learners to find out the name of a butterfly that lives in their local area and write its life cycle.

Name: _____

The life cycle of a butterfly

Complete this flowchart for the life cycle of a butterfly.
The first section has been done for you.

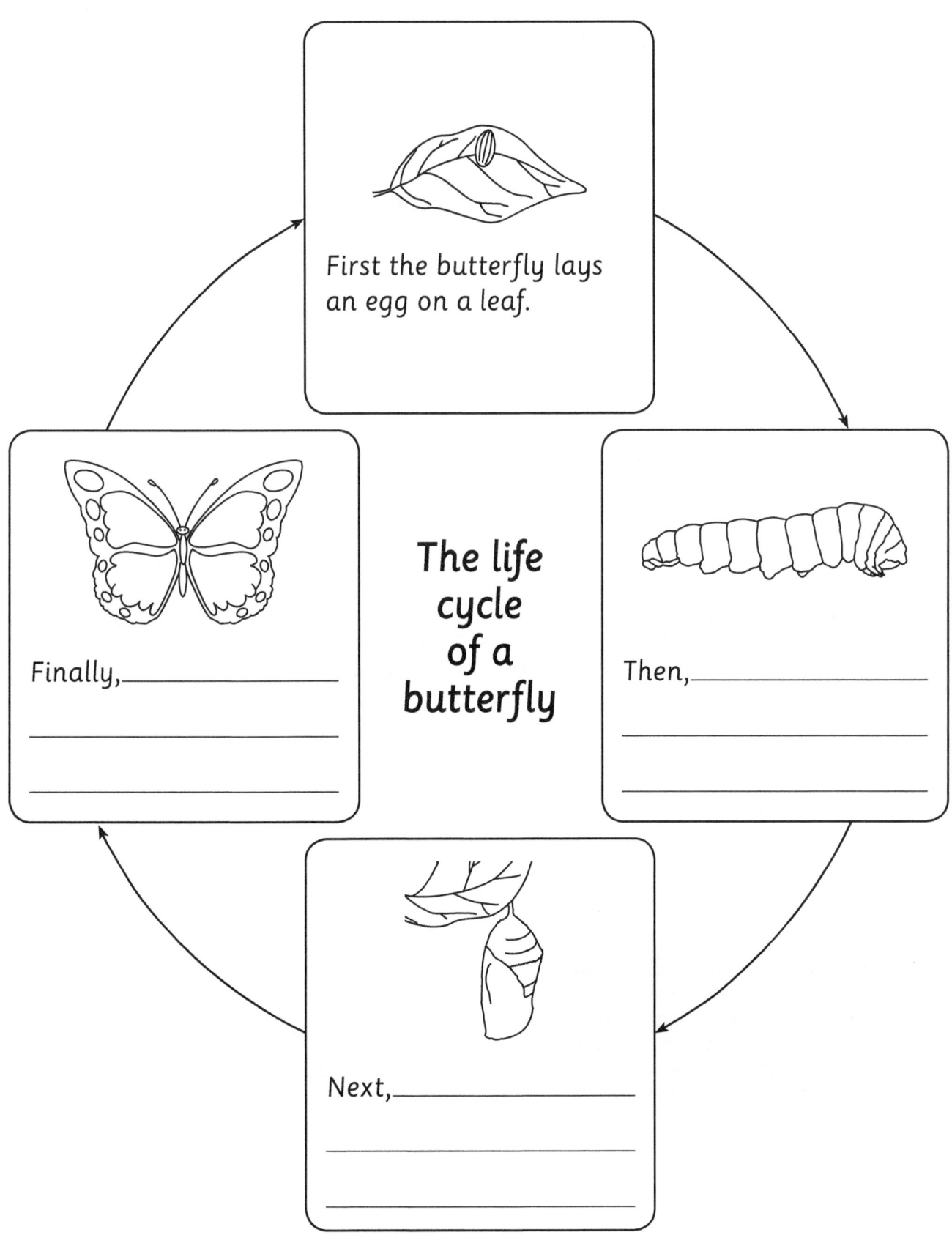

First the butterfly lays an egg on a leaf.

The life cycle of a butterfly

Then,_____

Finally,_____

Next,_____

The life cycle of a frog

Learning objectives

- Read and respond to question words, e.g. *what, where, when, who, why.* (2Rx1)
- Use past and present tenses accurately (if not always consistently). (2Wp4)
- Extend experiences and ideas through role-play. (2SL9)

Resources

Internet access; photocopiable page 103.

Starter

- Tell the learners that today they are going to write a flowchart for the life cycle of a frog. Ask: *What do you already know about the life cycle of a frog?* Ensure the learners know the meaning of any subject-specific words such as 'gills', 'lungs' and 'froglet'.

- Watch a film clip of the life cycle of a frog (there are many available on the internet, for example at www.youtube.com/watch?v=Hkyv_msRS6w). Warn the learners to concentrate because you will be handing out a quiz when it has finished.

Main activities

- Hand out photocopiable page 103 to the learners in small groups. Give the groups about 10 minutes to discuss and answer the questions.

- Discuss the answers – did any groups get all the answers right? Ensure full understanding of the life cycle before the learners move on to the next task.

- Ask the learners to create their own flowcharts that give an explanation of the four stages (eggs, tadpole, froglet, frog). Remind them of the tense, time words and connectives they should use. Provide them with a flowchart template by copying the flowchart from photocopiable page 101 with the images and text blanked out.

Plenary

- Ask the learners to role-play the different stages of this life cycle.
  - Stage 1: The learners cluster together to form a tight group.
  - Stage 2: The group breaks up into individual fish-like creatures (tadpoles), moving as fish.
  - Stage 3: The tadpoles lose tails and begin to hop around, still in the pond.
  - Stage 4: The frogs hop onto land and sit in the sun.

Success criteria

Ask the learners:

- Why was it useful to see a film of the life cycle of the frog?
- Why is it useful to break up the life cycle into four stages?
- What tense is an explanation written in?
- How did the role-play help you to understand the life cycle?

Ideas for differentiation

Support: Provide these learners with a set of pictures that show the different stages of the life cycle of a frog, and a set of simple captions to read and place by each stage.

Extension: Ask these learners to create a presentation on the life cycle of a frog.

Name: _____

A froggy quiz

Can you answer these questions about the life cycle of a frog?

1. What is the first stage of the life cycle of a frog?

    _____

2. Where do frogs lay their eggs?

    _____

3. Does the frog place them on a leaf, one by one, like the butterfly?

    _____

4. When does the second stage of the life cycle of a frog begin?

    _____

5. Why do tadpoles need gills?

    _____

6. Which other animals have gills?

    _____

7. What happens during the third stage of the life cycle of a frog?

    _____

8. What is a froglet?

    _____

9. What happens to the tail and the gills as the froglet grows?

    _____

10. What happens in the final stage of the life cycle?

    _____

The life cycle of a dinosaur

Learning objectives

- Use simple non-fiction texts as a model for writing. (2W04)
- Discuss the meaning of unfamiliar words encountered in reading. (2R10)
- Explore a variety of non-fiction texts on screen. (2R08)

Resources

Books and DVDs about dinosaurs; internet access; photocopiable page 105.

Starter

- Share a range of dinosaurs. Ask: *What do you know about dinosaurs?* If possible, try to use a range of sources – books, DVDs – for example *Walking with Dinosaurs* (BBC) or *Planet Dinosaur* (BBC), and the internet.
- Now explain that the learners are going to create a life cycle flowchart for a sauropod. Look at pictures of sauropods.

Main activities

- Display an enlarged version of photocopiable page 105 and read the information together with the learners. Explain what a fossil is.
- Hand out photocopiable page 105 to the learners in pairs and ask them to read it again and highlight any information they will need to create their flowchart.
- Help them to focus on the facts they will need by displaying the bare bones of the flowchart on the board. Give your flowchart a heading and three boxes (going round in a circle) headed 'Stage 1: Egg', 'Stage 2: Young' and 'Stage 3: Adult'. Leave plenty of room in your boxes to write.
- Call the class back together again and display an enlarged version of photocopiable page 105. Starting with Stage 1, ask the learners for information that might be useful. Look at the first three sentences and explain that they don't need all this information, although it is very interesting! Remind them that they must use the present tense and write a short sentence.

- Agree on a suitable sentence, for example: 'The sauropod lays an egg on the ground'.
- Ask them to draw their own flowchart and write their own version of this sentence for the first stage. Ask them to continue the task and complete the flowchart. Ask the learners to draw a labelled illustration for each stage. Provide them with access to books and the internet for further research.

Plenary

- Organise a table-top display for the learners' finished dinosaur flowcharts. Give each learner some sticky notes and ask them to use them to write positive comments on two or three flowcharts, for example: 'I liked your drawing because it showed how big the sauropods were.'

Success criteria

Ask the learners:

- What was the name of these dinosaurs?
- What new facts did you learn about dinosaurs?
- What is a fossil?
- How many stages are there in the life cycle of a dinosaur?

Ideas for differentiation

Support: Provide these learners with a sentence for each stage of the flowchart and ask them to position the sentences in the right boxes and illustrate them.

Extension: Challenge these learners to write a more detailed flowchart, adding what dangers a sauropod faced at each stage of its life.

Name: _____

Sauropods

Sauropods were the largest animals that have ever lived on Earth. They were a type of dinosaur and lived millions of years ago.

The sauropod females laid eggs in clusters on the ground. The clusters were then covered over to protect them. Each egg was shaped like a football, about 30 cm long and 25 cm wide. One fossilised egg found in Argentina was big enough to hold five and a half litres of water.

When they hatched the young dinosaurs grew quickly. To begin with they had feathers growing on their bodies.

All sauropods were plant eaters. Some sauropods had long, narrow teeth like pencils. They grabbed leaves from trees and swallowed them without chewing. Other sauropods had flatter teeth because they ate softer leaves. The adult sauropods had a very long neck. They could reach the highest trees and eat all day long. They also swallowed large stones to mash the leaves in their stomach!

Sauropods grew very fast, sometimes over 5 kg a day! Some sauropods grew very big: 25 m long and 15 m tall. Some of the bigger ones weighed the same as 14 elephants.

Diplodocus was a sauropod.

Dictionaries

Learning objectives

- Locate words by initial letter in simple dictionaries, glossaries and indexes. (2R09)
- Show some awareness that texts have different purposes. (2Rv1)
- Articulate clearly so that others can hear. (2SL3)

Resources

Simple dictionaries; a ball; a set of word cards; a set of CVC word cards; photocopiable page 107; paper strips.

Starter

- Show the learners a dictionary and ask: *What does a dictionary help us to do?* (Check the spelling of a word, find out the meaning of the word.) Ask: *How is it organised and why?*

- Recite the alphabet and play a range of games to practise alphabetical order.

- Play a game of 'Before or after': Sit in a circle with a ball. Throw the ball to a player opposite you and say, 'before c'. The learner must say 'b' and throw the ball to another player, saying 'before' or 'after' and a random letter. The new player must answer and the game continues. Encourage the learners to speak loudly and clearly.

Main activities

- Give each learner a dictionary and ask them to find the middle of their dictionary and mark it with their finger. Ask what letter of the alphabet features in this section. Then ask them to subdivide the two halves of the dictionary and mark these with their fingers. What letters appear on these quarter pages? Explain that they are holding the four quartiles of their dictionary. Help them to work out what letters the four sections cover.

- Call out one of your high-frequency words, for example 'said', and see how quickly the learners can find it in the dictionary using their knowledge of quartiles. Repeat with other words.

- Hand out photocopiable page 107 to each learner and ask them to complete the chart at the top before joining with a partner to play the 'Find the word' game, following the instructions.

Plenary

- Cut four long strips of paper of equal length to represent the quartiles of the class dictionaries. Write the letters in each quartile on one side and the heading 'First quartile', 'Second quartile', and so on, on the other side. Display the strips, heading side out, across the front of the classroom.

- Give every learner a word card. Tell them to come out when you call their name and stand by the quartile where their word is located. When everyone is at the front, turn over the heading to reveal the letters and ask them to work out if they are in the right place.

Success criteria

Ask the learners:

- What is a dictionary for?
- Why is it in alphabetical order?
- Can you find out how to spell a word by using a dictionary?
- Why are the quartiles useful for you if you need to find a word quickly?

Ideas for differentiation

Support: Help these learners to use an alphabet strip to place CVC words in alphabetical order then find them in the dictionary.

Extension: Give these learners a time limit to find a number of mathematical words in the dictionary.

Name: _____

The four quartiles of a dictionary

1. Write the letters of the alphabet from each quartile of your dictionary in the table below. The first one has been done for you.

2. Now write down any two words for each quartile.

Quartile 1	Quartile 2	Quartile 3	Quartile 4
a b c d			
apple crow			

Find-the-word game

You will need:

A partner and a dictionary.

What to do

- Call out one of your words above from any of the quartiles. Your partner has to find it in the dictionary as quickly as they can.

- Now your partner must call out one of their words and you must find it.

- See how quickly you can find all of your words!

Dictionary definitions

Learning objectives

- Use features of chosen text type. (2Wa5)
- Use simple non-fiction texts as a model for writing. (2W04)
- Begin to re-read own writing aloud to check for sense and accuracy. (2W03)

Resources

A set of picture cards; photocopiable page 109; simple dictionaries.

Starter

- Divide the learners into pairs and give a dictionary to each pair.
- Call out a word and tell the learners that as soon as they've found it they should leap to their feet and shout out the page number. Who can be the first?

Main activities

- Model writing a definition by selecting a simple picture card and talking through your thought processes, for example: *My picture shows a cat. A cat is small, it's a pet, and it's furry so I could write: 'cat: a small furry pet'. But, hold on a minute, that could be a mouse or a rabbit! I'll need to write what it looks like – it's got sharp claws, a long tail and small pointed ears. How about: 'cat: a small furry pet with sharp claws, a long tail and small pointed ears'? Those adjectives are really important to help describe a cat. I think that's a good definition – it makes sense and it's accurate.*
- Point to the way you have written the words and any punctuation you've used. Discuss any use of bold, dashes, colons, and so on. Explain that dictionaries are set out so that the key words are very easy to see as you scan your eye over the dictionary page.

- Ask different learners to come to the front and choose a picture card. Support the learners as they try to write a definition for the word.
- Hand out a set of picture cards to the learners in groups and ask them to take one card at a time, talk about its meaning and then come up with a definition. When they have written the definition, encourage them to re-read it and check it makes sense and describes the word.
- Write up a number of their definitions for the other learners to read and decide whether they make sense.
- Hand out photocopiable page 109 to each learner and ask them to complete the task.

Plenary

- Ask a learner to come to the front and choose a picture card without letting anyone see it. Ask them to describe the object to the rest of the class without using its name. How quickly can the rest of the class guess it?

Success criteria

Ask the learners:

- Why are the words in a dictionary written in bold print?
- What is a definition?
- Should a definition make sense?
- Why are adjectives important in a definition?

Ideas for differentiation

Support: Give these learners a set of pictures and simple definitions and ask them to match the pictures to the words.

Extension: Provide these learners with more difficult words to define, such as 'said', 'red', 'happiness'.

Name: _____

Dictionary definitions

Read the definitions below. Can you improve each one by adding more detail?

balloon: a small rubber bag

balloon: a small rubber bag that _____

_____

_____

giraffe: a tall animal

giraffe: a tall animal with _____

_____

_____

baby: a young child

baby: a young child that _____

_____

_____

carrot: an orange vegetable

carrot: an orange vegetable that _____

_____

_____

Using an index

Learning objectives

- Discuss the meaning of unfamiliar words encountered in reading. (2R10)
- Locate words by initial letter in simple dictionaries, glossaries and indexes. (2R09)
- Listen carefully and respond appropriately, asking questions of others. (2SL7)

Resources

A large number of information books with indexes; photocopiable page 109.

Starter

- Ask: *What is an index for?* Discuss the learners' answers and demonstrate how you can use the index to find information in a book.

- Give the learners in pairs an information book with an index. Explain that alphabetical order will help them find a word quickly, and demonstrate this: Say a letter of the alphabet and tell them to point to the words in the index starting with this letter.

- Ask the learners to take turns in their pairs to secretly choose a word from the index and then challenge their partner to find it and tell them the page number.

Main activities

- Ask the learners to look together at the index in their book and write down the six most interesting words that they see. Ask them to look up these words in the book, locate the word on the page and read the relevant information. Challenge them to use this information to write a question about each word, for example 'What is a quad bike?' or 'Where do pythons live?'

- Tell the learners to work together in this way until they have six interesting questions about their book. When they've finished, ask them to tuck their questions into their books and swap books with another pair.

- Now let the new pair use the index to find the answers to the questions in the book.

- Hand out photocopiable page 111 for the learners to complete a word search and create their own using the six words that they chose from their first book.

Plenary

- Share one of the books and its quiz with the whole class. Demonstrate finding the answers and congratulating the learners on their questions.

- Ask: *What is a contents list?* Discuss the differences between a contents list and an index and compare the two lists in a couple of books.

Success criteria

Ask the learners:

- Which types of books have an index?
- Why is alphabetical order used in an index?
- What is the purpose of an index?
- Does a contents page have a different purpose from an index page?

Ideas for differentiation

Support: Ask these learners to create an index of names of the learners in the class, using an alphabet strip as a check.

Extension: Provide these learners with a completed quiz without telling them which book it is from. Challenge them to quickly reject books as they fail to find the words in the index.

Name: _____

Word searches

1. Can you find these farming words in the word search?

> bonnet   farmer   hopper   furrow   barn

b	a	r	n	h	a	f
n	o	c	o	o	d	u
p	p	n	r	p	o	r
u	o	h	n	p	w	r
f	a	r	m	e	r	o
r	p	o	c	r	t	w

2. Make a list of words that you would like to hide in your own word search. Write them in the box below.

3. Now write the words in the grid below. They can go across, down or diagonally. Fill in the spaces with any other letters of the alphabet.

4. Challenge your partner to complete your word search!

Glossaries

Learning objectives

● Show some awareness that texts have different purposes. (2Rv1)

● Locate words by initial letter in simple dictionaries, glossaries and indexes. (2R09)

● Find factual information from different formats, e.g. charts, labelled diagrams. (2Rx4)

Resources

A large range of information books with glossaries; photocopiable page 113.

Starter

- Display a glossary from an information book and explain its purpose. Ask: *Why are the words organised alphabetically?* (To make them easier to find.)

- Read out some of the words in the glossary. Ask the learners to put their hands up when they want a word defined and pass them the book for them to read out the definition to the class. Ask: *Does that clarify the meaning of the word?*

- Now ask a volunteer to find the same word in the index and locate the right page to find the word. Ask them to read out the appropriate part of the text. Ask: *Do you now know how to use this new word?*

Main activities

- Hand out an information book with a glossary to the learners in pairs. Ask the learners in their pairs to repeat the activity above – reading definitions for unknown words and then seeing if they can understand the word in context when they find the word in the book using the index.

- Ask the learners to create a chart like this for the definitions they've investigated. Tell them to note if the glossary definition was clear or unclear.

Title of book	Word from Glossary	Page in book	Picture	Definition clear or unclear
TRACTOR	hopper	Page 8	Yes	Clear

- When each pair has done this for three words, call them back together as a class to discuss what they have done.

- Hand out photocopiable page 113 for the learners to complete individually.

Plenary

- Write out a number of glossary definitions and separate them into word and definition cards. Hand out the words and definitions to the learners and ask them to go round the classroom reading each other's cards until they have found their word if they're a definition or their definition if they're a word.

Success criteria

Ask the learners:

● Which type of books have glossaries?

● How is a glossary arranged so that it is easy to find the word you want?

● What is the purpose of a glossary?

● How could you find a picture to go with the word in the glossary?

Ideas for differentiation

Support: Write a set of simple definitions and have a set of pictures to match them. Ask these learners to read the definitions, find the pictures and stick these in alphabetical order.

Extension: Ask these learners to select an information book of their choice, find the glossary and select one word each, copying out the definition. They can read the definitions out and ask the class to guess their word.

Name: _____

Glossary game

Complete the table with the correct word and definition.
Choose from the words and meanings below.

Words

cruise ship   submarine   hovercraft   yacht

Definitions

a boat with a large sail

a ship that sails under the water

a large ship with restaurants and bedrooms that takes people on holiday

a ship that moves over water on a cushion of air

Word	Definition	Picture

Unit assessment

- Can you learn how something works by reading an explanation?
- Can you learn why things happen from an explanation?
- Can you explain how a flowchart works?

- What is a life cycle?
- Describe how to find your way around a dictionary.
- Why are indexes and glossaries arranged in alphabetical order?

Summative assessment activities

Observe the learners while they play these games. You will quickly be able to identify those who appear to be confident and those who may need additional support.

Using the four quartiles of a dictionary

This game assesses the learners' understanding of the four quartiles of the dictionary.

You will need:

Four sets of the words 'ambush', 'election', 'invade', 'noble', 'measles', 'reptile' and 'wharf' written on separate cards (replacing any words that do not occur in your call dictionary); four large cards with 'First quartile', 'Second quartile', and so on written on them, with the corresponding letters of the alphabet written around the heading; dictionaries.

What to do

- Divide the learners into four teams and give each team a set of words.
- Place each of the quartile signs in a different part of a room.
- Tell the teams that when they hear you say 'Go' they should spread the words out on the table, work out as a team which quartile of their dictionary the word would be found in and look it up. Whilst one team member runs to place the card by the correct sign, the others should read the dictionary definition aloud and try to remember it.
- The first team to correctly place all their cards is the winner, as long as they can correctly define each of the words.

True or false

This game assesses the learners' understanding of word definitions.

You will need:

A collection of words with their definition written on separate cards, with half of the definitions correct and half incorrect, for example 'Tractors: these are used to play on.', 'Ants: small insects that live in large groups.'

What to do

- Ask the learners to take a word, read the definition aloud to the class and then ask another learner if the definition is 'true' or 'false'.
- If the learner thinks the definition is 'false', they must say why.

Hand out photocopiable page 115 for the learners to complete individually. This activity will assess the learners' ability to write a simple, clear definition of a word they understand.

Name: _____

Definitions

1. Write a simple definition of a drum and draw a picture to illustrate your definition.

drum: _____

_____

2. Finish these definitions:

a) dinosaur: a large reptile _____

b) caterpillar: a long _____

c) egg: a young _____

'Magic horse'

Learning objectives

● Comment on some vocabulary choices, e.g. adjectives. (2Rw1)

● Choose interesting words and phrases, e.g. in describing people and places. (2Wa2)

● Vary talk and expression to gain and hold the listener's attention. (2SL4)

Resources

Photocopiable page 117; tinkling bells; internet access.

Starter

• Display photocopiable page 117 and explain that this poem is about a little girl having a dream that she is riding a magic horse that can take her to anywhere in the world!

• Wave the tinkling bells then read the poem.

• Ask the learners for their initial thoughts.

• Share pictures and films associated with the poem, including a black horse galloping (for example at www.youtube.com/watch?v=kaHtcrsvjyw).

Main activities

• Ask the learners to focus on the three lines that are repeated at the beginning of each verse. *Could they be how the little girl calls the magic horse to come and take her away to exciting places?*

• Ask the class to read these lines as if they can see the horse galloping around, holding their hands to their mouths and calling to attract its attention. Ask one group to read the first three lines like this, then the next four lines at a much faster pace.

• Talk about the line 'To the sandy beach'. Explain that using the adjective 'sandy' to describe the beach creates a clearer picture in their minds than just 'beach'. Model the effect of changing the adjective and then the noun to create a new line:

Across the bay
To the icy mountains,
Where I can play.

• Ask the learners to discuss with a partner all the places they would ask a magic horse to take them – both real and imaginary. When they're ready ask them to write their own version of the first verse using their dream destination, remembering to use an adjective to describe it.

Plenary

• Create a set of noun cards on paper of one colour and a set of adjective cards on another; ensure you have equal numbers of each. Give all the learners either an adjective or a noun. Ask the learners to go round the room combining adjectives and nouns, making note of all the combinations they create. Share the phrases they created and discuss which sound good and which sound odd, and which sound odd, but good.

Success criteria

Ask the learners:

● Which words help to create pictures in your mind?

● Why are the first three lines of 'Magic horse' repeated in every verse?

● How does using different expressions in your voice make the poem more interesting for listeners?

Ideas for differentiation

Support: Give these learners a set of pictures and adjectives on cards – ask them to select different adjectives to go with the pictures, and write a caption, for example 'a wide beach'.

Extension: Give these learners some travel brochures and ask them to find a picture and write a caption using adjectives to describe the picture.

Magic horse

Black horse,

Magic horse,

Carry me away,

Over the river,

Across the bay

To the sandy beach

Where I can play.

Black horse,

Magic horse,

Carry me away,

Over the seas

To the forest trees

Where I can watch

The tiger cubs play.

Black horse,

Magic horse,

Carry me away,

To Arctic snows

Where the cold wind blows

Where I can watch

The polar bears play.

Black horse,

Magic horse,

Carry me away,

To golden sands

In far away lands

Where the sea is blue

And I can play all day.

John Foster

Moon poems

Learning objectives

- Make simple inferences from the words on the page, e.g. about feelings. (2Ri3)
- Read aloud with increased accuracy, fluency and expression. (2RO6)
- Attempt to express ideas precisely, using a growing vocabulary. (2SL6)

Resources

Photocopiable page 118; a piece of fine net curtain; internet access.

Starter

- Tell the learners that they are going to read two poems about the moon.
- Read the 'Is the moon tired?' by Christina Rossetti from photocopiable page 119, softly and quietly, as it is a lullaby. Move your arm from east to west in an arc to explain the verb 'scales'.
- Ask: *What is the 'misty veil'?* Explain that in Christina Rossetti's day, women would often wear a veil to hide their faces when they were outside.
- Ask: *Why does the moon fade away?*
- Ask them to recite the poem softly and quietly as read by you. Listen to a version read aloud on the internet (for example at www.youtube.com/watch?v=2igq-qoOp10).

Main activities

- Organise the learners into small mixed-ability groups and give each group photocopiable page 119. Ask a learner from each group to read 'Someone' to the rest of their group.
- Ask: *Who is the 'someone'?* (The Moon.) *Who is the 'round red face'?* (The Sun.)
- Ask: *How does the poet try to make 'Someone' scary?* (By saying that there's someone outside looking in; he hasn't eyes, a nose or a mouth; the light comes 'stealing in' like a thief; repetition of 'Not a single hair'.)

- Ask: *Why does the moon disappear?* Ask the learners to compare this with Christina Rossetti's poem.
- Model how to write a simple list poem about the moon, thinking of adjectives and arranging them poetically, for example:

Moon	Moon
White	Ashen
Papery	Whitish
Icy	Pale
Cool	Lifeless

- Ask the learners to write their own list poem about the moon.

Plenary

- Draw two large circles on the board – one for the moon and one for the sun. Ask the learners to suggest scary words for you to write in the moon circle and happy words for the sun. Model making up a simple poem using the words – a verse for the moon and a verse for the sun. Ask for a brave volunteer to create a line or two for each.

Success criteria

Ask the learners:

- Why did Christina Rossetti say the moon wore a veil in 'Is the moon tired'?
- Why does Gareth Owen say the moon has a face in 'Someone'?
- Do you think Gareth Owen might have been scared of the moon when he was little?

Ideas for differentiation

Support: Divide these learners into two groups and ask each group to learn one verse of 'Is the moon tired?' and perform this for the class.

Extension: Ask these learners to use the words from the Plenary to write a poem about the Moon and the Sun.

The Moon

Is the moon tired?

Is the moon tired? She looks so pale

Within her misty veil;

She scales the sky from east to west,

And takes no rest.

Before the coming of the night

The moon shows papery white;

Before the dawning of the day,

She fades away.

Christina Rossetti

Someone

There's a white-faced someone at my window

Watching me lying in bed

He hasn't an eye or a nose or a mouth

Not a single hair on his great white head.

Not a single hair on his head.

The light from his face comes stealing

Across the bed where I lie

But he just disappears when daylight appears

And another round face fills the sky

Yes, a round red face fills the sky.

Gareth Owen

'Two friends'

Learning objectives

- Demonstrate 'attentive listening' and engage with another speaker. (2SL8)
- Extend experiences and ideas through role-play. (2SL9)
- Use features of chosen text type. (2Wa5)

Resources

Photocopiable page 121; rhyming dictionaries or internet access.

Starter

- Tell the learners that you are going to read a poem by Julia Donaldson, the author of *The Gruffalo.*
- Display a large version of the first verse on photocopiable page 121 and read it. It should make the learners laugh! Ask them to join in as you read it again.
- Talk about the nouns that create exact pictures of where Lily lives and what she does, for example the shoebox, the tin, the acorn cup, the raindrops, the greenfly and the nutshell. Ask the learners to turn to a partner and role-play being a tiny person – what do they use for a car, for going on holiday; what's it like in the garden?
- Talk about the rhyming pattern in the poem (tin / pin; cup / up) and the cheerful fun beat.

Main activities

- Display the second verse of the poem and ask the learners to join in as you read it.
- Point out the similes in the opening lines of both verses, and explain that similes compare one thing to another.
- Ask the learners to write a two-line poem that starts with a simile, for example: 'My friend Dave is as brave as a lion / His head's made of concrete and his fist's made of iron!'

- Display a list of the following similes for the learners to choose from, or they can make up their own:

as brave as a lion	as busy as a bee
as gentle as a lamb	as quick as lightning
as happy as a lark	as good as gold
as pretty as a picture	as light as a feather
as hard as nails	as funny as a circus
as strong as an ox	as sweet as honey

- Encourage the learners to try lots of different options before settling on their favourite.
- Help them to use rhyming dictionaries to extend their word choices (for example at www.poetry4kids.com/modules.php?name=Rhymes&op=searchy).
- Share the poems as a class.

Plenary

- Display one of the poems and with the learners change the noun in the simile, for example: 'as hard as … rocks, ice, concrete, steel' or 'as sweet as … jam, sugar, cake, ice-cream'. How does the change in noun change the feel of the simile?

Success criteria

Ask the learners:

- Why does Lily choose a greenfly as a pet in 'Two friends'?
- Which nouns describe the huge things Trudy uses?
- How does a simile help make a picture of someone in your head?

Ideas for differentiation

Support: Ask these learners to think of some other tiny pets Lily might have and draw a picture of her, writing a simple caption about why she likes these pets.

Extension: Ask these learners to create another pair of rhyming lines to continue their poem.

Two friends

My friend Lily is as little as a pin.

She lives inside a shoebox. She
  sleeps inside a tin.

When her plates are dirty she
  takes an acorn cup

And fills it full of raindrops to do
  the washing up.

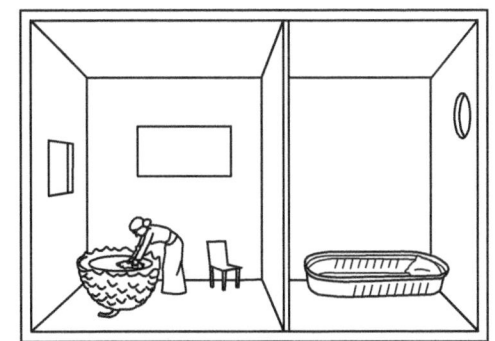

She likes to play with greenfly; she keeps one as a pet

And she puts it in a nutshell when she takes it to the vet.

I wanted mum to meet her, so I asked her home to tea

And she ran about the table playing football with a pea.

My friend Trudy is taller than a tower

And once she picked a tree because she thought it was a
  flower.

She has skipping ropes for laces on her size 100 feet

And when she needs to blow her nose
she blows it on a sheet.

She takes a lamp-post up to bed to keep
  away the dark

And she says she keeps a tadpole but
  I'm certain it's a shark.

She came to lunch and ate it with a
  garden fork and saw,

Then she snapped a drainpipe off the
  house and used it as a straw.

Julia Donaldson

Aliens

Learning objectives

- Comment on some vocabulary choices, e.g. adjectives. (2Rw1)
- Vary talk and expression to gain and hold the listener's attention. (2SL4)
- Choose interesting words and phrases, e.g. in describing people and places. (2Wa2)

Resources

Photocopiable page 123.

Starter

- Tell the learners that they are going to learn a very short poem called 'Three cheers'. Warm up by getting them to shout 'Hip hip hooray!' three times.
- Display the poem on photocopiable page 123 and read it once, saying the first two lines with urgency, the second two lines in a serious voice and the final lines in a happy voice – then call out for the learners to give three cheers, as it says in the final line.
- Hand out individual copies of photocopiable page 123 and ask the learners to work in small groups to learn the poem by heart, reading it with expression, as you have modelled. Explain that reciting a poem helps us to appreciate the style, rhyme and meaning of a poem.

Main activities

- Read 'The alien' aloud to the learners and then ask them to join in with a second reading.
- Challenge the learners to draw a quick sketch of this alien.
- Ask them why the alien was laughing at the human who had seen him. (Perhaps because a human would have looked like a very strange alien.)

- Ask the class to write their own version of this poem by changing just a few words. Model how to do this:

The alien
Was as round as the moon.
Well, he could be as round as an orange, as the sun, as an apple …
Let's change it to
The alien
Was as round as the **sun**
Let's change how many legs he has to three
Three legs he had
Let's get something else playing a tune
Toes *instead of ears*
And his toes played a tune.
Let's change the colour of his hair to purple
His hair was purple
Now let's read our new poem!

- Tell the learners that if they feel more adventurous they can have a go at changing other lines.

Plenary

- Ask the learners to get into pairs and say the poem 'Three cheers' together, and then draw a smiley face or a sad face, depending on how well they thought they varied the tone of their delivery.

Success criteria

Ask the learners:

- Who did the monster spot from the planet Venus in 'Three cheers'?
- Can you find the five adjectives used to describe this monster?
- Could humans appear funny to aliens?

Ideas for differentiation

Support: Support these learners to create a simple description of an alien for the written activity, rather than use the structure of the poem.

Extension: Ask these learners to write a second verse for 'Three cheers'.

Alien poems

Three cheers

I think we've been spotted from Venus;

A big bug-eyed monster has seen us.

It's fierce and it's red

With great horns on its head.

Three cheers for the distance between us!

Barry Buckingham

The alien

The alien

Was as round as the moon.

Five legs he had

And his ears played a tune.

His hair was pink

And his knees were green,

He was the funniest thing I'd seen.

As he danced in the door

Of his strange spacecraft.

He looked at me –

And laughed and laughed!

Julie Holder

List poems

Learning objectives

- Discuss the meaning of unfamiliar words encountered in reading. (2R10)
- Build and use collections of interesting and significant words. (2Wa3)
- Use the structures of familiar poems and stories in developing own writing. (2W05)

Resources

Photocopiable page 125; thesauruses; (video) camera.

Starter

- Display the poem 'Ten thing to eat beginning with G ...' from photocopiable page 125. Read it aloud, then ask the learners to join in.
- Tell them that the words beginning with 'G' are nouns – naming words. Ask them to think of food they eat beginning with another letter, for example 'P'.
- Model writing a new list poem using these new words.
- Ask the learners what the purpose of this poem is. (To have fun with words, to learn new words, to create word pictures.)

Main activities

- Display the second poem 'Eleven words to use instead of said ...' and read it aloud. Explain the meaning of any words the learners may not be sure of, for example 'drone' (go on and on and on about something). Point out that these words are all verbs.
- Have fun by asking the learners in pairs to show the meaning of a word by either making an appropriate noise (grunt, yell, snivel, groan, squeal) or saying something to show what the word means (mumble 'sorry I'm late').
- Tell them that using different verbs like these in their writing, rather than using 'said' all the time improves their writing.

- Demonstrate this by writing up a straightforward sentence on the board, for example: '"I'm going home," she said'. Then replace the verb 'said' with different verbs, demonstrating how much more effective they can be. Talk about how different verbs will also need different punctuation, for example an exclamation mark or question mark.
- Ask the learners to work in pairs to write a new list poem called 'Six more words to use instead of said ...', using a thesaurus if they run out of ideas.
- Call the class together to share their poems. If possible, film different learners reciting their poems to share with other classes.

Plenary

- Display this sentence: 'The man walked down the road'. Circle the word 'walked'.
- Give the learners in pairs an alternative word for 'walked'.
- Ask a pair of learners to come out to the front. Ask one learner to read the new sentence and the other to mime the meaning of the word as the sentence is being read.

Success criteria

Ask the learners:

- Do these poems rhyme?
- What is the purpose of list poems?
- Could children learn new verbs by reading the poem 'Eleven words to use instead of said ...'?
- Why are these poems easy to write?

Ideas for differentiation

Support: Ask these learners to write another list poem: 'Six things to eat beginning with T'.

Extension: Ask these learners to write another list poem: 'Eleven words to use instead of big'.

Wonderful words

Ten things to eat beginning with G ...

grape

greengage

groundnut

gooseberry pie

gravy

garlic ice-cream

ginger biscuit

goulash

Granny Smith apple

Garibaldi biscuit

Judith Nicholls

Eleven words to use instead of said ...

mumble

grumble

mutter

drone

grunt

stutter

yell

moan

snivel

groan

squeal

Judith Nicholls

Funny poems

Learning objectives

● Write using a variety of sentence types. (2Wp6)

● Choose interesting words and phrases, e.g. in describing people and places. (2Wa2)

● Recount experiences and explore possibilities. (2SL1)

Resources

Photocopiable page 127.

Starter

• Display an enlarged version of photocopiable page 127 and read 'Colour' to the class. Ask the learners to join in with you as you read it again.

• Cover up the colours in the poem and ask the learners to think about different colours they might use.

• Then ask selected learners to call out different colours for each line to create a different poem based on the original. Remind them that colours are adjectives.

• Compare the original poem with the new one they have created – which one do they like best?

Main activities

• Read aloud 'I know someone' from photocopiable page 127.

• Ask the learners which line is repeated over and over, then point out that the pairs of lines read together make a sentence. Explain that this poem is a set of sentences.

• Give some examples of sentences like this that describe a learner in your class, for example:
  • I know someone who can run very fast.
  • I know someone who can play the piano.

• Give them some examples of sentences that describe fantastic things that someone can do, for example:
  • I know someone who can walk backwards up a mountain.
  • I know someone who can juggle with 100 balls.

• Show them how these sentences could be laid out as in the original version:
  I know someone who can walk backwards up a mountain.

• Ask the learners to get into small groups and think of sentences based on their own experiences or about someone they know – or just think up something fantastic!

• Ask them to sit in a circle and take it in turns to say a sentence for the poem.

• Ask the learners to write a poem of their own with a minimum of three sentences.

Plenary

• Write up three different sentence beginnings and ask the learners in groups to take turns to think of an ending that would make sense.
  • I know someone who …
  • I know why …
  • I know where …

Success criteria

Ask the learners:

● Do poems have to rhyme?

● Can a poem just be a set of sentences?

● Do adjectives create pictures in our mind that we could draw?

● Did you write sentences about something you could really do?

Ideas for differentiation

Support: Provide these learners with different endings to choose from and draw a picture to go with them (for example: 'who can do ten forward rolls up a hill?'; 'who can eat ten ice creams in one go?').

Extension: Ask these learners to choose a favourite superhero and use the format 'I know someone who can …' to write a poem about them.

Funny poems

Colour

Take a brush:

the sky is green

the grass is blue

you are purple

the house is silver

the sun is black

the river is gold

the world has changed.

Did you do that?

Michael Rosen

I know someone

I know someone who can make their

ears wiggle.

I know someone who can shake their

cheeks so it sounds like ducks quacking.

I know someone who can throw peanuts

in the air and catch them in their mouth.

I know someone who can bend her

thumb back to touch her wrist.

I know someone who can say the

alphabet backwards.

I know someone who can wiggle her

little toe.

And that someone is me.

Michael Rosen

Unit assessment

Questions to ask

- Why is it important that the poets chose the best adjectives and nouns in the poems in this unit?
- What is the purpose of Christina Rossetti's poem 'Is the moon tired?'
- Which poet used similes to describe a tiny girl and a gigantic girl?
- Can you describe the aliens in the poems 'Three cheers' and 'The alien'?
- Do the list poems by Judith Nicholls make you think of interesting words?
- Can you remember one of the sentences you wrote for your poem called 'I know someone who can'?

Summative assessment activities

Observe the learners while they play these games. You will quickly be able to identify those who appear to be confident and those who may need additional support.

Adjectives game

This game helps to assess the learners' understanding of the power of adjectives.

You will need:

Adjectives from photocopiable page 129, cut into cards – enough for every learner to have a card.

What to do

- Sit the learners in a circle and give each learner an adjective card.
- Ask the first learner to say their word aloud. The next learner must then think of a phrase that uses the adjective, for example: 'a black mountain', 'cold hands', 'golden beaches', and so on.
- If a learner has the same card as someone that has gone before, they must think of a new phrase.

Simile match

This activity helps to assess the learners' understanding of common similes.

You will need:

Simile halves from photocopiable page 129, cut into cards – enough for every learner to have a card (ensuring that you have both halves of each simile).

What to do

- Give each learner a simile part and tell the learners to walk round classroom reading each other's cards until they find their pair.
- Ask them to sit down as a pair when they have completed their simile.
- Ask the pairs to join with another pair and take turns to mime their simile to the other pair. Can the other pair guess the simile?

List poem

This game helps to assess the learners' ability to group words to create a simple list poem.

You will need:

Sets of words and phrases relating to familiar themes, for example: 'food', 'the beach', 'playing in a park', and so on.

What to do

- Hand out mixed-up sets of words to the learners in pairs.
- Ask them to sort words into lists that go together, for example '10 things to eat beginning with the same letter', '10 things to do at the beach'.

Written assessment

Ask the learners to think of ten words to describe someone who is very special to them, for example a parent, sibling, friend or grandparent. These might include words such as: lovely, kind, funny, and so on. Ask them to write these as a list poem.

Word cards

Adjectives game

black	cold	golden
pale	misty	dirty
five	blue	yellow
sandy	strange	pink

Simile match

as warm as	toast
as tall as	a house
as flat as	a pancake
as proud as	a peacock
as quiet as	a mouse
as green as	grass
as thin as	a rake
as smooth as	glass

George and the Dragon

Learning objectives

- Identify and describe story settings and characters, recognising that they may be from different times and places. (2Ri2)
- Predict story endings. (2Ri1)
- Write using a variety of sentence types. (2Wp6)

Resources

Internet access; *George and the Dragon* by Chris Wormell (Red Fox); photocopiable page 131.

Starter

- Ask: *What do you know about dragons? Do they really exist? Did they ever exist? What kinds of stories do we find dragons in?*
- Look at images of dragons on the internet and watch a film clip of an animated dragon roaring (for example at www.youtube.com/watch?v= g3BGbwwDgjc&feature=related).
- Display the front cover of *George and the Dragon*.
- Encourage comments on the artwork (colour, detail, size, facial expression, and so on). Ask the learners to tell you what they notice about the dragon (for example the slight hint of smoke drifting from its nostrils, the angry look in its eyes, the sharp teeth and powerful claws, the long tail, the huge wings, the sharp spines on its back claws).
- Display the back cover and encourage the learners to give you some adjectives to describe the high mountains.

Main activities

- Read the opening pages, drawing the learners' attention to the long opening sentence and repetition of adjectives for effect.
- Point out the author's clever use of descriptive verbs and adjectives: 'a *blast* of his *fiery* breath', 'a *flick* of his *mighty* tail', 'a *sweep* of his *monstrous* wing'. Ask the learners to mime these three phrases individually and in small groups.

- Hand out individual copies of photocopiable page 131 and ask the learners to create some dramatic sentences for another monster story. Afterwards, share these together.
- Return to *George and the Dragon* and read up to 'His name was George'. Ask: *How might this story end?*

Plenary

- Encourage the learners to join in with their best scary voices with the following classic story: 'In a dark, dark forest, there was a dark, dark house. And in that dark, dark house, there was a dark, dark staircase. Up the dark, dark staircase there was a dark, dark door. And through the dark, dark door there was a dark, dark room. In the dark, dark room there was a dark, dark cupboard. And in that dark, dark cupboard there was a dark, dark box. And in that dark, dark box there was … A GHOST.'

Success criteria

Ask the learners:

- Why was it surprising to have a mouse as a main character in this book?
- How do you predict the story might end?
- What did you enjoy about writing different types of sentences like those the author used?

Ideas for differentiation

Support: Provide these learners with some words and phrases to choose from for photocopiable page 131.

Extension: Ask these learners to write their own story opener about the sea monster, in the style of *George and the Dragon*, but without using the photocopiable page.

Name: _____

In a dark, dark cave

eyes as big as footballs   long, sharp pointed beak   large, dark cave

saucer-shaped suckers filled
with razor-sharp teeth

Look at the picture of the sea monster above, then finish these
opening sentences for a story about it. Use powerful words that
will make your classmates afraid!

Far, far away in the deep, _____ ocean, in a _____

_____, there lived a _____

monster.

He could swim faster than _____.

He could cut up a _____ with his _____

_____.

He could frighten off a hundred sharks with his _____.

There was nothing as _____ as this _____

sea monster!

The Dragon's problem

Learning objectives

- Discuss the meaning of unfamiliar words encountered in reading. (2R10)
- Make simple inferences from the words on the page, e.g. about feelings. (2Ri3)
- Link ideas in sections, grouped by content. (2Wt3)

Resources

George and the Dragon by Chris Wormell (Red Fox); photocopiable page 133.

Starter

- Re-read *George and the Dragon* by Chris Wormell up to 'His name was George', encouraging the learners to join in the reading with fluency and expression.
- Ask: *How is the story going to end?* Make a list of their ideas.
- Finish reading the story, explaining any difficult words ('draughty', 'fixtures', 'inconvenient') and information (that bats hang upside down to sleep and rest).
- Now compare the ending with the learners' own ideas of how this story might have ended.

Main activities

- Ask the learners to get into small discussion groups and spend time discussing the following questions:
  - *What do you think the princess felt when the dragon captured her?*
  - *How do you think George felt when the dragon appeared to be really terrified of him?*
  - *How did the dragon feel about himself before George arrived?*
  - *How did the dragon feel about himself after George arrived?*
  - *Is George a calm and sensible mouse?*
  - *What does he say that tells you he is not scared of the dragon?*
  - *Is the princess a calm and sensible person?*
  - *Is the dragon a calm and sensible creature?*

- Call the learners together again and share their views and opinions.
- Hand out photocopiable page 133 and ask the learners to complete the activity independently. This will give them the opportunity to group information about the three characters.

Plenary

- Organise the learners into the roles of the dragon, the princess and George. Ask them to go around the room having conversations with their classmates in role.
- Ask different learners questions about their character and behaviour in the story, telling them to answer the question in role. Ask two or three learners the same questions to elicit slightly different answers. Give the learners feedback on the way they answer these questions, both in respect of answering in role and their understanding of the story.

Success criteria

Ask the learners:

- Can you remember the meaning of 'fixtures and fittings'?
- How do we know the dragon was terrified of mice?
- What did George say and do that showed he was not frightened of the dragon?
- Did going in role as the dragon make you feel sorry for him?

Ideas for differentiation

Support: Give these learners a smiley face, a sad face and a picture of each of the three characters. With the assistance of an adult helper, ask them to choose a face to match each character in turn at different points in the story, and discuss their answers.

Extension: Ask these learners to write another long sentence about a power that the dragon has that is not mentioned in the book.

Name: _____

Preparing for role-play

What do you know about the three characters in
George and the Dragon by Chris Wormell? Write about:

- what they look like

- what they like

- what they do not like

- whether or not they are brave.

What I know about the dragon:

_____

_____

_____

_____

What I know about George:

_____

_____

_____

_____

What I know about the princess:

_____

_____

_____

_____

Retelling *George and the Dragon*

Learning objectives

● Begin to use dialogue in stories. (2Wa4)

● Begin to re-read own writing aloud to check for sense and accuracy. (2W03)

● Show awareness that speakers use a variety of ways of speaking in different situations and try out different ways of speaking. (2SL11)

Resources

Group copies of *George and the Dragon* by Chris Wormell (Red Fox); photocopiable page 135.

Starter

• Tell the learners that *George and the Dragon* is a very popular book and children love it because it is exciting and fairly easy to remember.

• Organise the learners into small groups and give each group a copy of *George and the Dragon*. Challenge them to learn the story off by heart as a group, practising several times to make sure they are word perfect.

• Ask each group in turn to perform the story. Ask the listeners to give the group marks out of five for:
  • knowing the words
  • performing the story in an engaging way.

Main activities

• Explain to the learners that they are now going to write their own version of the story, starting in a different way this time – this new story is going to start with the dragon talking about his powers. Ask the learners to describe the powers the dragon might boast of at the beginning of the story and make a list. Encourage them to think as widely and creatively as possible, so that you have an extensive list for them to draw from later.

• Model how to begin writing this opening, talking about speech punctuation and the use of exclamation marks to show how boastful he is: '"I am a fierce, terrible and mighty dragon!" said the dragon. "I can fly higher than the clouds and faster than birds! I can wipe out an army with a flick of my wrist."'

• Hand out individual copies of photocopiable page 135 and ask the learners to write their version of the story, using the class list to inspire them to write the dragon's opening boast.

• When the learners have finished writing their stories, ask them to read them aloud to their partner to check for sense and accuracy, making changes if necessary.

Plenary

• Provide the learners with copies of the following sentences and ask them to punctuate them correctly before reading them aloud to their partner with expression, using a variety of ways of speaking:
  • I am the most powerful dragon in the land everyone is frightened of me muttered the dragon
  • when will I ever find a new home in this cold and windy place asked George

Success criteria

Ask the learners:

● What punctuation shows that a character is speaking?

● Did your story make sense when you read it aloud?

● What difference did it make to the dialogue when you spoke in different ways?

Ideas for differentiation

Support: Ask these learners to tell their version of the story to an adult helper who can scribe for them.

Extension: Ask these learners to continue the story with the next section starting 'One year later ...'

Name: _____

Story planner

Use this grid to tell your own version of **George and the Dragon**.

George and the Dragon
Beginning: The dragon boasts about his powers!
George arrives.
George needs sugar.
What happens next.
Ending: The tea party.

The Smartest Giant in Town

Learning objectives

● Identify and describe story settings and characters, recognising that they may be from different times and places. (2Ri2)

● Use phonics as the main method of tackling unfamiliar words. (2RO2)

● Read and respond to question words, e.g. *what, where, when, who, why.* (2Rx1)

Resources

The Smartest Giant in Town by Julia Donaldson (Macmillan); internet access; photocopiable page 137.

Starter

• Display the front and back cover of *The Smartest Giant in Town.* Allow a few minutes for the learners to gaze at the pictures and talk about what they see. Ask: *Where is this story set? Who will the characters be? Who might the legs belong to?*

• Ask the learners to read the title by putting together the letter sounds, self-correcting the initial letter 'G' into the /j/ sound (or help them to do this).

Main activities

• Read the story up to where George gives one of his socks to the fox or watch a film clip of the first half of the story (for example at www.youtube.com/watch?v=_S2Y-z0jzWw).

• Without further discussion, hand out photocopiable page 137 to the learners in pairs. Ask them to read and discuss the questions together. Call the class back together to share their answers.

• Ask the learners to think of words to describe George (nice, kind, caring, loving, generous, helpful, unselfish, and so on). Ask if they could suggest another title for this book using one of these words instead of 'smartest'.

• Ask the learners to tell you the events that have happened so far in the book, in the right order. Write these up in a story map representing the journey George takes; draw pictures with captions for each event, for example:
  ◦ George feels scruffy so he buys some new clothes. (Picture of the shop.)
  ◦ George meets the giraffe and gives him his tie to warm his neck. (Picture of the giraffe.)

Plenary

• Ask every learner to write down a question about the book, which begins with either 'Who', 'What', 'Where', 'When', 'Why' or 'How'. Arrange the learners into two lines facing each other – Line A and Line B.

• Tell the first learner in Line A to read out their question to the first learner in Line B, who then has to answer it and then ask their own question to the second learner in Line A, who should answer it and ask their question to the second learner in Line B, and so on.

Success criteria

Ask the learners:

● Where is this story set?

● Which event starts the whole story?

● What follows on from that?

● Did you find the questions easy or hard to answer? Say why.

Ideas for differentiation

Support: Provide these learners with a set of answers for photocopiable page 137 and help them to decide which one would fit where.

Extension: Ask these learners to write answers to this question: 'Do you think you could learn anything important from this story?'

Talking about the story

Read these questions about **The Smartest Giant in Town** by Julia Donaldson with your partner and discuss the answers.

1. Who is George?

2. What does the word 'scruffiest' mean?

3. How does George feel about being scruffy?

4. What does the word 'smart' mean?

5. Which new clothes does George buy?

6. Why does George give his tie to the giraffe?

7. What does the goat want?

8. How does George replace the house for the mice?

9. Who tells George about his wish for a dry sleeping bag?

10. What have you learnt about George the giant?

Learning more about George

Learning objectives

- Begin to read with fluency and expression, taking some notice of punctuation, including speech marks. (2R07)
- Find answers to questions by reading a section of text. (2Rx3)
- Extend experiences and ideas through role-play. (2SL9)

Resources

Internet access; multiple copies of *The Smartest Giant in Town* by Julia Donaldson (Macmillan); photocopiable page 139; large card, large envelope and a gold paper crown.

Starter

- Sing the version of the song in *The Smartest Giant in Town* that George sings after he's given his sock to the fox. Use any tune you like and sing it happily.
- Work through the song line by line, asking the learners to talk about each event in turn, referring to the story map started in the previous lesson.

Main activities

- Read aloud or listen to the second half of the story (for example at www.youtube.com/watch?v=k0whQAknJgE).
- For dramatic effect, write the song from the last page onto a large piece of card and place it in an envelope with a gold paper crown. Bring this out at the appropriate point in the story and share it with the learners before leaving it on display.
- Continue drawing the story map representing George's journey, with captions for each event, for example: 'George helps the dog', and so on.
- Sing the final version of the song together with the learners. Ask them about the ending of the book and George's final attitude to his clothes.

- Work with the learners in pairs, supporting them as they read *The Smartest Giant in Town* aloud together, taking note of the speech marks and using different voices for George and the animals, taking on different roles between them.
- Hand out individual copies of photocopiable page 139 and a copy of the book to the learners in pairs. Ask them to discuss the characters in turn, using the book as reference, before filling in the photocopiable page independently.

Plenary

- Choose different learners to take on the role of each character and to come out in turn to sit in the hot seat. Encourage the other learners to ask the character interesting questions, for example (to the goat): 'Why did you go sailing on a stormy day?' or 'Couldn't you have bought a new sail?'

Success criteria

Ask the learners:

- Did you find it easy to read and sing George's song?
- Is it more interesting to listen to someone reading if they use different voices for characters?
- Did you enjoy taking part in the hot-seating session?

Ideas for differentiation

Support: Help these learners with photocopiable page 139 by preparing a sentence about each character, which they have to read, cut out and stick into the correct boxes.

Extension: Ask these learners to move beyond what they know about the characters from the book to create realistic back stories for each one.

Name: _____

Looking at characters

Write everything you know about these characters from
The Smartest Giant in Town by Julia Donaldson.

George	_____ _____ _____
The giraffe	_____ _____ _____
The goat	_____ _____ _____
The mouse	_____ _____ _____
The fox	_____ _____ _____
The dog	_____ _____ _____

Using adjectives

- Comment on some vocabulary choices, e.g. adjectives. (2Rw1)
- Build and use collections of interesting and significant words. (2Wa3)
- Write using a variety of sentence types. (2Wp6)

The Smartest Giant in Town by Julia Donaldson (Macmillan); photocopiable page 141; pairs of opposite adjectives (long / short, and so on) written on cards; adjective cards and picture cards.

Starter

- Tell the learners that they are going to learn more about adjectives and build up a collection of interesting words to use in their writing.
- Write the following sentence on the board: 'Fred was a frog'.
- Explain that this sentence tells us very little about Fred, apart from the fact that he is a frog. Now write it again in the style of Julia Donaldson: 'Fred was a frog, the slimiest frog in the pond'. Point out how the adjective 'slimiest' paints a much better picture of Fred.
- Model how to write another sentence in this style. 'Jacob was a boy, the messiest boy in town'.

Main activities

- Display the page in *The Smartest Giant in Town* that shows the new clothes that George buys. Point out that some of the phrases under the clothes have only one adjective – 'smart' – in them.
- Ask the learners to work in pairs to think of a couple of adjectives to add to 'smart' in each case, for example 'a smart shirt': 'a new, white shirt'. Share the learners' ideas and create a list of all the new adjectives they have suggested ('beautiful', 'classy', 'sharp', 'glamorous', 'showy', 'trendy', 'up-to-date', 'stylish', and so on).

- Write the sentence 'I have a long, warm scarf' on the board. Point out the two adjectives – 'long' and 'warm'. Ask the learners to write another sentence like this, about a hat they have, for example 'I have a red, furry hat.'
- Hand out photocopiable page 141 to each learner and ask them to use their imagination to complete the sentences.
- Call the learners back together and select a number of sentences to read aloud. Discuss how the adjectives create word pictures.

Plenary

- Give each learner a card with two opposite adjectives on it, for example 'long / short'. Ask the learners to create a sentence using both their adjectives, for example 'My trousers are too long but my brother's are too short.'

Ask the learners:

- Which adjective describes George after he has visited the clothes shop?
- Say why the phrase 'smart shiny shoes' is better than 'black shoes'.
- Were your sentences more interesting when you used adjectives?

Support: Hand out a set of picture cards and a set of adjectives and ask these learners to make up short sentences by matching adjectives to a picture.

Extension: Ask these learners to think of a toy they would really like to have and describe it, using lots of adjectives to create a picture in the minds of their listeners.

Name: _____

Interesting adjectives

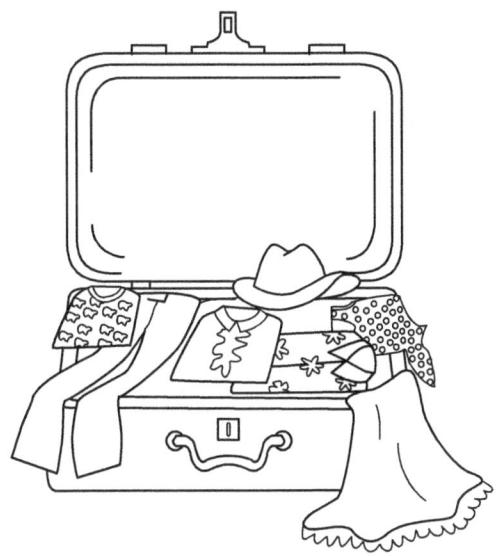

Create word pictures by using adjectives to describe a suitcase of old clothes you found in the attic. Choose adjectives from the box below or think of your own.

spotty	frilly	techni-coloured	old-fashioned
enormous	tiny	broken lacy	pretty long
short	dusty	black	gold flowered

1. The straw hat was _____, _____ and

    _____!

2. The cricket shoes were _____, _____ and

    _____!

3. The shirt was _____, _____ and

    _____.

4. The trousers were _____ and _____.

5. The skirt was _____ and _____.

6. The _____ was _____ and

    _____.

Using time words

- Find alternatives to *and / then* in developing a narrative and connecting ideas. (2Wp2)
- Use the language of time, e.g. *suddenly, after that.* (2Wt2)
- Choose interesting words and phrases, e.g. in describing people and places. (2Wa2)

Resources

Photocopiable page 143; *The Smartest Giant in Town* by Julia Donaldson (Macmillan).

Starter

- Display the final version of George's song in *The Smartest Giant in Town* by Julia Donaldson and ask the whole class to sing it together.
- Tell the learners that they are going to write their own version of the story of *The Smartest Giant in Town.*
- Display the completed story map from the first two lessons in this chapter, and ask the class to read the events aloud.

Main activities

- Write the following on the board: 'George bought some new clothes and then he met a giraffe and then he met a goat and then he met a mouse.'
- Point out that using 'and then, and then' is really boring! Ask the learners to suggest other time words that move a story along. ('One day ...', 'As ...', 'Later on ...', 'Soon after ...', 'Then ...', 'Next ...', 'Now ...', 'When ...', and so on).
- Give each learner photocopiable page 143 and ask them to read it aloud.
- Discuss how this version of the story covers all the plot but lacks drama. Ask: *How can we make this story more interesting?* Discuss how they could add some adjectives to describe the animals as George meets them.

- Write the name of each animal on the board and ask the learners to suggest different adjectives for each animal. Model using adjectives suggested for the giraffe in a sentence, for example: 'As he left the shop he met a **tall**, **sad** giraffe who needed a scarf, so he gave him his tie'.
- Encourage the learners to write their own version of the story, adding adjectives and detail to the sentences provided on photocopiable page 143. Remind them to re-read their writing as they go along.

Plenary

- Share the different stories that the learners have written. Encourage the learners who are listening to carry out the actions from photocopiable page 143 as they listen.

Success criteria

Ask the learners:

- Why is it a good idea to stop writing 'and then, and then,' in stories?
- Can you think of some time words to use in stories?
- Why is it a good idea to use adjectives in stories?

Ideas for differentiation

Support: Provide a storyboard with eight boxes on a large piece of paper and ask these learners to cut out and stick the text from photocopiable page 143 in the right order and illustrate each event in the story.

Extension: Ask these learners to write a short review of *The Smartest Giant in Town* that could persuade a learner from another class to read the book, beginning: 'You will love this book! It tells the story of ...'

And now with actions

Use this simple version to help you retell **The Smartest Giant in Town** by Julia Donaldson with actions. Add some interesting adjectives to give drama to the story.

Story	Actions to mime
One day, George the giant felt really scruffy so he went into town to buy new clothes. He bought a shirt, trousers, a belt, a tie, socks and shoes.	Make a circle with your hands to open the story, and say all the text aloud.
As he left the shop he met a giraffe who needed a scarf, so he gave him his tie.	taking off a tie
Later on he came to a river. Here he met a goat who needed a sail so he gave him his shirt.	wiggling your fingers like waves taking off a shirt
Soon after he met a mouse whose house had burned down, so he gave her a shoe.	taking off a shoe
Then he met a fox who was crying. He needed a sleeping bag so George gave him a sock.	crying taking off a sock
Next he met a dog who was stuck in the mud. So he gave him his belt for a path through the mud.	being stuck in the mud taking off a belt
Now George needed more clothes so he went to the shop but it was closed and he started crying. George found his old smock.	crying putting on a smock
When he got home the animals gave him a crown and he put it on.	putting on a crown
	Everyone sing the song.

The Snail and the Whale

- Identify and describe story settings and characters, recognising that they may be from different times and places. (2Ri2)
- Explain plans and ideas, extending them in the light of discussion. (2SL2)
- Begin to re-read own writing aloud to check for sense and accuracy. (2W03)

Internet access; several copies of *The Snail and the Whale* by Julia Donaldson (Macmillan); a globe or map of the world; photocopiable page 145.

Starter

- Introduce *The Snail and the Whale.*
- Ask the learners what they know about whales and sea snails. If possible, show them images and film clips from the internet of humpback whales leaping from water and of a giant sea snail moving. Tell the learners that whales move from warm water in the winter for breeding to colder water in the summer for feeding. Use a globe or a map to point out the warmer areas where they can be found in the winter: Hawaii, Australia and the Caribbean. Point out the colder areas where they feed in the summer: Alaska, Antarctica and New England.

Main activities

- Display the cover of *The Snail and the Whale,* showing the picture of the whale. Ask the learners to describe what they see in the cover picture that tells them the whale is in a warm place (toucans, parrots, monkey, lizard, flying fish, warm sandy beaches). These images mean the cover picture probably shows somewhere in the Caribbean.
- Explain any unusual words and phrases from the book before you read it, for example 'itchy foot' (a desire to travel). Make a connection between the phrase 'itchy foot' and the fact that a snail travels on just one foot!

- Read the whole book, and ask the learners to talk about what they liked in the story.
- Tell them that whales frequently get washed up on beaches and have to be rescued.
- Give each learner photocopiable page 145 to complete. Ask them to re-read their own writing to make sure that it makes sense and includes everything that happened during the rescue.

Plenary

- Prepare a number of statements based on the book (for example: 'Snails have two feet.', 'Snails travel.', 'Having an itchy foot means you should scratch it.', 'Snails can write.', 'Whales sing.') Organise the learners into small groups and give each group a set of statements. Allow them five minutes to decide if each statement is true or false.
- Check all answers to see which group has the most correct.

Ask the learners:

- Where do you think the setting for this story might be?
- Explain what you enjoyed when writing about the rescue of the whale.
- Why do you think that re-reading your writing is important?

Support: Help these learners with photocopiable page 145 by giving them a selection of sentence finishers that they can choose from.

Extension: Ask these learners to find out information about how a real whale can be saved, using the internet.

Name: _____

The plan

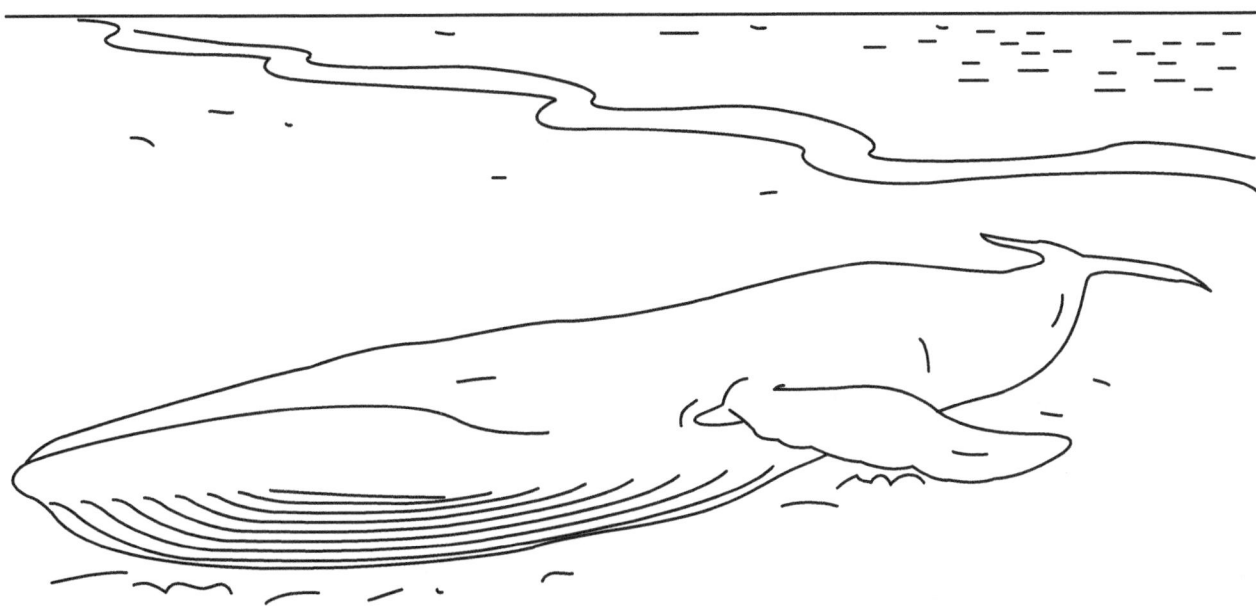

Complete this description of how the whale was saved.

The snail rushed off to the _____

_____

The children rushed off to fetch _____

_____

They all started to dig a _____

_____

The firemen sprayed _____

_____

The tide came in _____

_____

How the whale was saved

Learning objectives

- Extend experiences and ideas through role-play. (2SL9)
- Make simple inferences from the words on the page, e.g. about feelings. (2Ri3)
- Begin to vary sentence openings, e.g. with simple adverbs. (2Wp5)

Resources

Several copies of *The Snail and the Whale* by Julia Donaldson (Macmillan); individual copies of filled-in photocopiable page 145; photocopiable page 147.

Starter

- Choose a few learners to read out their description on photocopiable page 145.
- Ask the other learners to listen carefully and if a sentence doesn't make sense to ask the reader to clarify what they mean.

Main activities

- Tell the learners to get into small groups and ask them to discuss the answer the snail would give to these questions. Provide each group with a copy of the book.
  - *Why would anyone like to visit the icy world of Antarctica?*
  - *Why do you think volcanoes are so terrifying?*
  - *What did you enjoy about the splashing of the waves?*
  - *What did you feel when you first saw the sharks?*
  - *How did you manage to stay on the whale's tail without falling off?*
  - *How did you know what to do to save the whale?*
  - *Why were you happy that lots of your snail friends came with you on your next journey with the whale?*
- Choose a learner from each group to go into role as the snail. Ask each 'snail' one of the questions they have already discussed. In each case, ask the other 'snails' if they have anything to add.

- Give feedback to the learners on the way they have thought about and discussed the questions.
- Re-read the first page of the book to the learners, putting particular expression into how the snail is feeling. Ask the learners to tell you which words show that she desperately wants to travel the world.
- Model how to write a sentence beginning with an adverb, for example 'Longingly, she thought about how she would love to see the world.'
- Ask the learners to complete photocopiable page 147.

Plenary

- Provide the learners, working in teams, with a long list of verbs that suggest positive or negative feelings. Ask the teams to sort out the positive (for example 'happy') from the negative (for example 'angry') verbs.

Success criteria

Ask the learners:

- Was it interesting to get ready for the role-play as the snail by thinking about the answers to questions that would be asked?
- What have you learnt about the feelings of the snail from the words on the page?
- Can you think of a sentence that starts with the word 'Sadly'?

Ideas for differentiation

Support: Ask these learners to write a few captions about the whale – what he really enjoyed doing and why.

Extension: Ask these learners to write a few sentences about why the whale decided to take the snail with him.

Name: _____

Starting sentences with adverbs

Choose an ending from this box to finish the sentences below.

> she crawled to find help for the stranded whale.
>
> she clung to the whale in the stormy seas.
>
> she watched the sharks swim by.
>
> she let the waves splash and spray her with foamy water.
>
> she gazed at the sky, the sea and the land.

1. Happily, _____
   _____

2. Fearfully, _____
   _____

3. Desperately, _____
   _____

4. Contentedly, _____
   _____

5. Bravely, _____
   _____

Interesting adjectives

Learning objectives

- Choose interesting words and phrases, e.g. in describing people and places. (2Wa2)
- Find alternatives to *and / then* in developing a narrative and connecting ideas. (2Wp2)
- Begin to re-read own writing aloud to check for sense and accuracy. (2W03)

Resources

The Snail and the Whale by Julia Donaldson (Macmillan); photocopiable page 149.

Starter

- Start this lesson by explaining that in *The Snail and the Whale* Julia Donaldson makes excellent use of adjectives in her writing.
- Distribute *The Snail and the Whale* so that all the learners can see a copy. Go through the book page by page and, with the help of the learners, make a list on the board of all the adjectives used in the story. Leave the list on display.

Main activities

- Ask the learners to imagine that the snail decides to write the story of her travels with the whale, using adjectives and adverbs to create descriptions of where she went.
- Display an enlarged copy of photocopiable page 149, which has the bare bones of the snail's adventures on it. (The sentence openers will avoid the learners writing 'and then, and then'.)
- Model completing parts of the story, providing the learners with lots of options:
  - *First of all we travelled through cold seas where I saw [towering icebergs, penguins staring, smooth seals gazing …]*
  - *Next we saw [sunny beaches, crawling turtles, flying fish, dolphins leaping …]*
  - *And heard [a volcano exploding, chattering monkeys, talking parrots]*
  - *Sometimes the waves were [scary, frightening, and sometimes they were fun …]*

- *Once we swam under the sea and I was scared when we saw [scary sharks, a green octopus, crabs with big claws …]*
- Encourage the learners to use the detail in Alex Scheffler's illustrations of *The Snail and the Whale* for inspiration as they write. Tell them to use the adjective list to help them create interesting sentences.
- Remind them to re-read their writing as they go along, instead of at the end. Develop this practice by moving around groups, asking individual learners to read their writing to you and offer constructive comments. Praise the incorporation of descriptive sentences and phrases.
- Ask the learners to draw an illustration for their finished story.

Plenary

- Arrange a table-top display where the stories and pictures are shown side by side. Invite the learners to move around in groups, enjoying reading the other learners' stories.

Success criteria

Ask the learners:

- How does Julia Donaldson create word pictures to describe places?
- Why is it not a good idea to join all the sentences in a story together with 'and then'?
- Did you check your writing to make sure that it made sense?

Ideas for differentiation

Support: Ask these learners to draw a snail and label it with interesting adjectives.

Extension: Ask these learners to write without using the story frame; expect a high level of descriptive language.

Name: _____

Story planner

Complete this account by the snail of her journey with the whale.

My travels with a whale

I have always wanted to travel the world so when I saw a huge whale floating in the sea I wrote a message on a rock asking for a lift.

First of all we travelled through cold seas where I saw _____

_____

Next we saw _____

_____

and heard _____

_____

Sometimes the waves were _____

_____

Once we swam under the sea and I was scared when we saw _____

_____

A bad thing happened when the whale _____

_____

I decided to _____

_____

Before long _____

_____

Finally, we arrived home and the snails _____

_____

Comparing two books

Learning objectives

- Identify general features of known text types. (2Rv2)
- Begin to develop likes and dislikes in reading and listening to stories drawing on background information and vocabulary provided. (2R05)
- Write simple evaluations of books read. (2Wa7)

Resources

Photocopiable page 151; simple stick puppets of George, the snail and the whale; several copies of *The Smartest Giant in Town* and *The Snail and the Whale* by Julia Donaldson (both Macmillan); other books by Julia Donaldson.

Starter

- Tell the learners that in this final lesson they will compare *The Smartest Giant in Town* with *The Snail and the Whale*. They can then decide which book they like best, and why.
- Show the learners an enlarged copy of photocopiable page 151 and talk them through it, explaining that they must give reasons for their opinions in each box.
- Hold up the stick puppets of George, the snail and the whale and role-play them, saying in turn: *I'm sure that you will think that I am the most interesting character in the book!*
- Organise the learners into small groups and ask the groups to discuss each character in turn, saying something positive about each one. Give each group a copy of *The Smartest Giant in Town* and *The Snail and the Whale* to refer to.

Main activities

- Ask the groups to compare the covers of the two books and discuss the different settings. Ask them to look through both books and discuss how many different settings that can find in each one.

- Briefly discuss the story of each book, asking for help from the learners.
- Hand out individual copies of photocopiable page 151 and ask the learners to complete the page using their own opinions. Remind them that they also need to say why they think what they think.
- Call the class together. Write up the names of both books on the board and start a tally system for the titles as each learner tells you their opinions for each element.

Plenary

- Divide the learners into two teams and ask questions about different aspects of the two books, for example:
  - Character: *Who can look right over houses? Who wants to see the world?*
  - Setting: *Where does George meet the goat?*
  - Story: *How does the whale get stranded?*

Success criteria

Ask the learners:

- Who is a brave character in these stories?
- Who goes on a journey to town and the countryside?
- Which story do you prefer – and why?

Ideas for differentiation

Support: Arrange for an adult helper to work with these learners to help them compose their answers to photocopiable page 151 by orally telling the adult helper what they will write.

Extension: Ask these learners to choose another book by Julia Donaldson and compare it to *The Snail and the Whale* and *The Smartest Giant in Town*.

Name: _____

My opinion

Use this table to compare **The Smartest Giant in Town** with **The Snail and the Whale** by Julia Donaldson.

Characters
The Smartest Giant: I think he is _____
_____
because _____
_____
The snail: I think she is _____
_____
because _____
_____
The whale: I think the whale is _____
_____
because _____
_____
My favourite character is _____
because _____
_____
Setting
The setting I like best is the _____
because _____
Story
The story I like best is _____
because _____

Unit assessment

- Can you explain who George is in *George and the Dragon* by Chris Wormell and why he terrifies the dragon?
- Are the illustrations important in this book?
- Can you explain who another George is in another book, and why he does not terrify anyone?

- As whales and snails are real creatures, is *The Snail and the Whale* by Julia Donaldson story true or made up?
- What do you think people could learn from *The Snail and the Whale*?

Summative assessment activities

Observe the learners while they play these games. You will quickly be able to identify those who may need additional support.

Picture this

This activity assesses how quality illustrations give information and extend understanding.

You will need:

Several copies of *George and the Dragon* by Chris Wormell (Red Fox); *The Smartest Giant in Town* and *The Snail and the Whale* by Julia Donaldson (both Macmillan).

What to do

- Divide the learners into four mixed-ability groups; work with each group in turn.
- From *George and the Dragon* display: the cover, the first picture of George and the last two pages. Ask: *Why do you like these pictures? Can you say what is happening?*
- Award one point for a correct answer and two points for a more detailed answer (for example giving interesting views).
- From *The Smartest Giant in Town* display: the cover, meeting the goat and the last two pages. Use the same questions and points system. Award bonus points for any answer that compares these illustrations to the illustrations of *George and the Dragon*.
- From *The Snail and the Whale* display: the cover, the double page spread of the storm and the last two pages. Use the same questions and points system.
- When all four groups have completed the activity, compare points.

Adjective game

This game assesses the learners' word skills, for example the meaning and use of a wide range of adjectives.

You will need:

The following nouns on cards (multiple copies – one for each learner): waves, mountain, sea, sky, volcano; the following adjectives displayed on the board: gigantic, towering, crashing, frightening, icy, treacherous, velvety, star-studded, twinkling, sparkling, vast, enormous, beautiful, incredible, amazing, stunning, turbulent, boiling, eerie, sinister.

What to do

- Sit the class in a circle.
- Hand out the set of nouns on cards, enough for every learner to have one. Ensure that all the learners can see the adjectives displayed.
- Ask the first learner to create a sentence by using their noun and one of the adjectives, for example: 'The waves looked like boiling water!'
- Award points for each sentence: 1 = good; 2 = fantastic!
- When everyone has had a go, swap the noun cards around and go round the circle again.

Hand out photocopiable page 153 to each learner. Read through this story opening together and ask the learners to finish the sentences to make sense.

Name: _____

A whale's story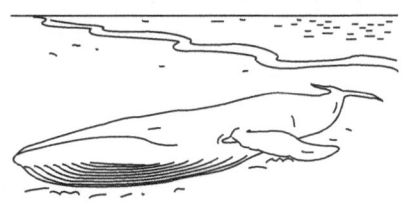

1. The whale from **The Snail and the Whale** by Julia Donaldson
    is talking about his travelling life. Finish the sentences for him.

    a) 'I am a humpback whale and I love my life as I swim from
        warm to cooler seas.

        In cooler seas I see _____

        _____

    b) In warmer seas I see _____

        and I hear _____

        _____

    c) Sometimes the waves _____

        _____

    d) In caves below the waves I see _____
                                                                    '
        and _____

2. Draw a picture to show the cave you have described.

3. Pretend you are a deep-sea diver who is swimming through this cave.
    Write what you can see.

    _____

    _____

    _____

Non-chronological reports

Learning objectives

- Identify general features of known text types. (2Rv2)
- Show some awareness that texts have different purposes. (2Rv1)
- Write simple evaluations of books read. (2Wa7)

Resources

A range of information, instruction, poetry and story books – enough for one for each learner; sticky notes; four hoops labelled 'Information', 'Instructions', 'Poetry' and 'Story'; photocopiable page 155; a simple information book for each learner; a number of dice.

Starter

- Ask the learners to sit in a circle, and place a selection of books (enough for one for each learner) and the four labelled hoops in the middle of the circle.
- Explain to the learners that the books need to be sorted. Model doing this for one of the books, for example: *This is a book about tractors – it's all about how tractors work and the jobs they do. I'm going to place it in the hoop labelled 'information'.*
- Ask the learners to work together to organise the pile of books into the four hoops.

Main activities

- Muddle up the books again and give them out randomly to each learner.
- Ask the learners to decide if their book is an information, instruction, poetry or fiction book. Hand out sticky notes and ask the learners to write the text type on a sticky label and stick it to the front of their book.
- Organise the learners into groups and tell them to share their books in turn within their groups, saying what type of book it is and explaining why they think so. The rest of the group should then say if they agree or not.

- Ask the learners to place their books back in the hoops.
- When they've finished, go through the books in each hoop in turn, checking that they are correctly filed. Talk about the purpose of the different types of text as you check.
- Hand out individual copies of photocopiable page 155 for the learners to complete. Call the class back together again and share what they have written.
- Hand out a simple information book to each learner and allow them time to read through their book and complete the sentence: 'What I liked about this book …' Ask them to locate one interesting fact in their book.

Plenary

- Organise the learners into small groups and give each group a dice. Ask the groups to take it in turns to roll the dice, telling them that if they roll a six they should introduce their information book, read out their evaluation sentence and share their interesting fact.

Success criteria

Ask the learners:

- Can you think of two types of books that might have imaginary creatures in them?
- If you wanted to learn how to build a wall, what type of book would you choose?
- What is the purpose of an evaluation of an information book?

Ideas for differentiation

Support: Place these learners in a mixed-ability pair to read and discuss their simple information books.

Extension: Provide these learners with more complicated information books to work with.

Name: _____

Text type detective

Read each text below and decide which type of book it comes from – choose from the list below. The first one has been done for you.

| story | poem | instruction | information |

Text	Text type
A hermit crab finds an empty shell, moves into it and makes it his new home.	Information
Once upon a time there was a boy called Jack. He lived with his mother in a small cottage.	
Tractors can harvest carrots. The carrots are pulled up, their tops cut off, and they are dropped into a trailer.	
Beat the butter and sugar together, then add the egg.	
At seven, when I go to bed, I find such pictures in my head: Castles with dragons prowling around, Gardens where magic fruits are found.	
The river that contains the most water is the Amazon in South America.	

Using an index and glossary

Learning objectives

- Locate words by initial letter in simple dictionaries, glossaries and indexes. (2R09)
- Discuss the meaning of unfamiliar words encountered in reading. (2R10)
- Make simple notes from a selection of non-fiction texts, e.g. listing key words. (2W07)
- Articulate clearly so that others can hear. (2SL3)

Resources

A selection of information books that have index and glossary pages; set of 'Search and Find cards' (see below); photocopiable page 157.

Starter

- Recap on the purpose and features of an index and a glossary in an information book.
- Remind the learners that both are arranged in alphabetical order because this makes the words quicker to find. Choose an information book and demonstrate finding a word in the glossary and index.
- Read out a few definitions from the glossary.

Main activities

- Create a simple 'Search and find' card for each of the information books you plan to use in this session, for example:

Search and find: Sea creatures

Find these words in the index and then turn to the right page in the book. Write down the page number and one fact about each subject.

Starfish:

Clam:

- Hand out a selection of information books with a 'Search and find' card inside each one to the learners in pairs.
- Allow ten minutes for the learners to find the words on the card.

- Hand out individual copies of photocopiable page 157 for the learners to complete.
- Hold a quick quiz at the end of the lesson, asking questions such as: *What is algae? Is seaweed a type of algae?* Tell the learners that they must speak clearly when giving the meanings of these words so that everyone can understand.

Plenary

- Display the following statements and ask the learners to agree or disagree with each one, explaining why:
  - An index is found at the end of a story book.
  - A glossary is found at the beginning of an information book.
  - These words are in alphabetical order: octopus, crab, antennae.
  - A glossary explains the meaning of more difficult words.
  - Information books contain lots of facts that you may not know.

Success criteria

Ask the learners:

- Why are indexes arranged in alphabetical order?
- Why are glossaries needed in information books?
- Tell me a new word you have learnt today.

Ideas for differentiation

Support: Arrange for an adult helper to work with these learners when they are finding words and reading the meaning so that they can write at least one fact.

Extension: Ask these learners to find a book about undersea creatures, read the glossary and add new questions for the quiz.

Name: _____

Learning new words

1. Read the definitions of these words.

> **Algae:** a type of plant. Seaweeds are types of algae.
>
> **Antennae:** feelers that a creature uses to sense where it is or to find food.
>
> **Coral:** a colony of tiny animals called polyps that live in a bony structure that they create. Millions of coral polyps join together to form a coral reef.
>
> **Suckers:** cup-shaped pads that stick to surfaces used by creatures to stick to things around them.

2. Now write the correct word next to each picture below.

	_____
	_____
	_____
	_____

Writing information

● Use features of chosen text type. (2Wa5)

● Use simple non-fiction texts as a model for writing. (2WO4)

● Begin to re-read own writing aloud to check for sense and accuracy. (2WO3)

Internet access; photocopiable page 159.

Starter

• Tell the learners that the writing in most information books is in the form of a non-chronological report. Reports have many facts that are true (unlike stories, which are made up). These types of reports often have lots of photographs that show you what something is really like.

• Display a simple double-page spread from an information book. As you talk through it, point out the features of this type of report:
  • A heading at the top: *This tells the reader what the report will be about.*
  • Sentences written in the present tense: *Non-chronological reports usually describe the way something is.* (If appropriate, explain that this is not true for history books, or reports of other events that happened in the past.)
  • *Sentences often have more than one fact in them.*

• When you have finished reading the report, conceal it and see how many facts the learners can remember.

Main activities

• Explain that the learners are now going to write their own report about a crab. Display an enlarged copy of photocopiable page 159. Explain that this gives lots of facts about pie-crust crabs, but these facts are presented in note form as a bullet-point list. The job for the learners is to turn this information into a report.

• Ask the learners if they have ever eaten a pie with pastry on the top? Explain that the pie-crust crabs are so called because their shells look just like pastry on a pie with fork marks around the edge! If possible, show photographs of pie-crust crabs from the internet.

• Hand out photocopiable page 159 to each learner and model how to start off the report: *I'll put the heading at the top: 'Pie-crust crabs'. Now I must remember to use the present tense, so I'm going to write: 'Pie-crust crabs are found in New Zealand and Australia.'*

• Tell the learners to write the reports individually, checking that their writing is accurate and makes sense. Call the class together and read out selected reports.

Plenary

• Place a range of statements about the pie-crust crab, some true and some false, in a hat (for example: 'A pie-crust crab's shell is made by a cook.', 'These crabs eat vegetables.', 'Its mouth is very sharp, like a knife.'). Select different learners to take a question from the hat, read it out and then ask the rest of the class to vote if the statement is true or false.

Ask the learners:

● Is a report written in the past tense?

● Why do reports often have photographs?

● Did you have to change your writing because it did not make any sense?

Support: Prepare a ready-made report with missing key words that these learners can fill in using the fact box on photocopiable page 159.

Extension: Ask these learners to research a different crab, for example the hermit crab, and present a short report about it to the class.

Name: _____

Writing a report

Pie-crust crabs – factfile

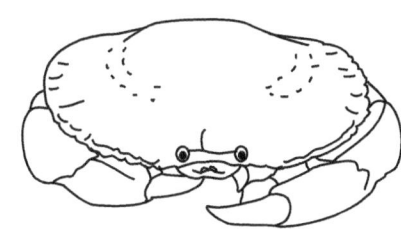

- Found in New Zealand and Australia
- Top part of shell looks like pie crust
- Brownish colour helps it hide among pebbles
- Two huge pincers
- Shell 15 cm wide
- Eats shrimps and mussels
- Bites through shells with very sharp mouth
- Female crab lays 3 000 000 eggs in lifetime
- Only a few eggs survive to be adults

Use the information above to write your own report about the pie-crust crab. Don't forget to give your report a heading.

_____

_____

_____

_____

_____

_____

Finding information from a chart

Learning objectives

- Find factual information from different formats, e.g. charts, labelled diagrams. (2Rx4)
- Explore a variety of non-fiction texts on screen. (2R08)
- Demonstrate 'attentive listening' and engage with another speaker. (2SL8)

Resources

Internet access; information books about bats; photocopiable page 161; a globe or world map.

Starter

- Ask: *Have you ever seen a bat? What do you know about bats?*

- On a poster-sized piece of paper write the heading 'What we already know about bats' and write down everything that the learners tell you about bats. Display the poster.

- Visit a few internet sites about bats together (for example www.bbc.co.uk/nature/life/Bat or bats4kids.org). Gather together some information books about bats and allow time for the learners to look at these in groups.

Main activities

- Show an enlarged version of the fruit bat on photocopiable page 161 (with the labels hidden) and introduce the fruit bat.

- Ask the learners to name the body parts, and reveal the boxes to show the words.

- Ask the learners to look at the chart. Explain the meaning of the word 'habitat' (where a creature lives). Read through the chart, focusing on one bat at a time. Show the learners where these bats live using the globe or map.

- Ask: *Why are charts like these a useful way of displaying information?* (Lots of information can be displayed easily; can display similar information side-by-side, and so on.)

- Ask the learners to work in pairs and give each pair photocopiable page 161. Ask them to use the chart to answer the following questions, discussing the answers together first before writing them down:
  - *Which is the smallest bat?*
  - *Where does it roost?*
  - *What does it eat?*
  - *Where does a fruit bat roost?*
  - *How big is it?*
  - *Does it eat spiders?*
  - *How does a vampire bat feed?*
  - *Which dark places does it like to roost in?*
  - *How big is it?*

Plenary

- On another large piece of paper write 'What we have learnt about bats' and ask the learners to tell you what they have learnt about bats in this lesson (from the books, the internet or photocopiable page 161). Write these facts under the heading.

- Is there anything that the learners thought they knew about bats that they now know to be wrong (for example that bats are blind, that vampire bats suck blood, and so on)?

Success criteria

Ask the learners:

- Which do you prefer: information from books or from the internet?
- Why is a labelled diagram useful?
- Why is it important to listen to each other when working together to answer questions?

Ideas for differentiation

Support: Support these learners as they locate the answers to the questions.

Extension: Give these learners a cut-up version of the chart with 12 pieces of information and see if they can re-assemble it with the correct information in place.

Bats

The fruit bat

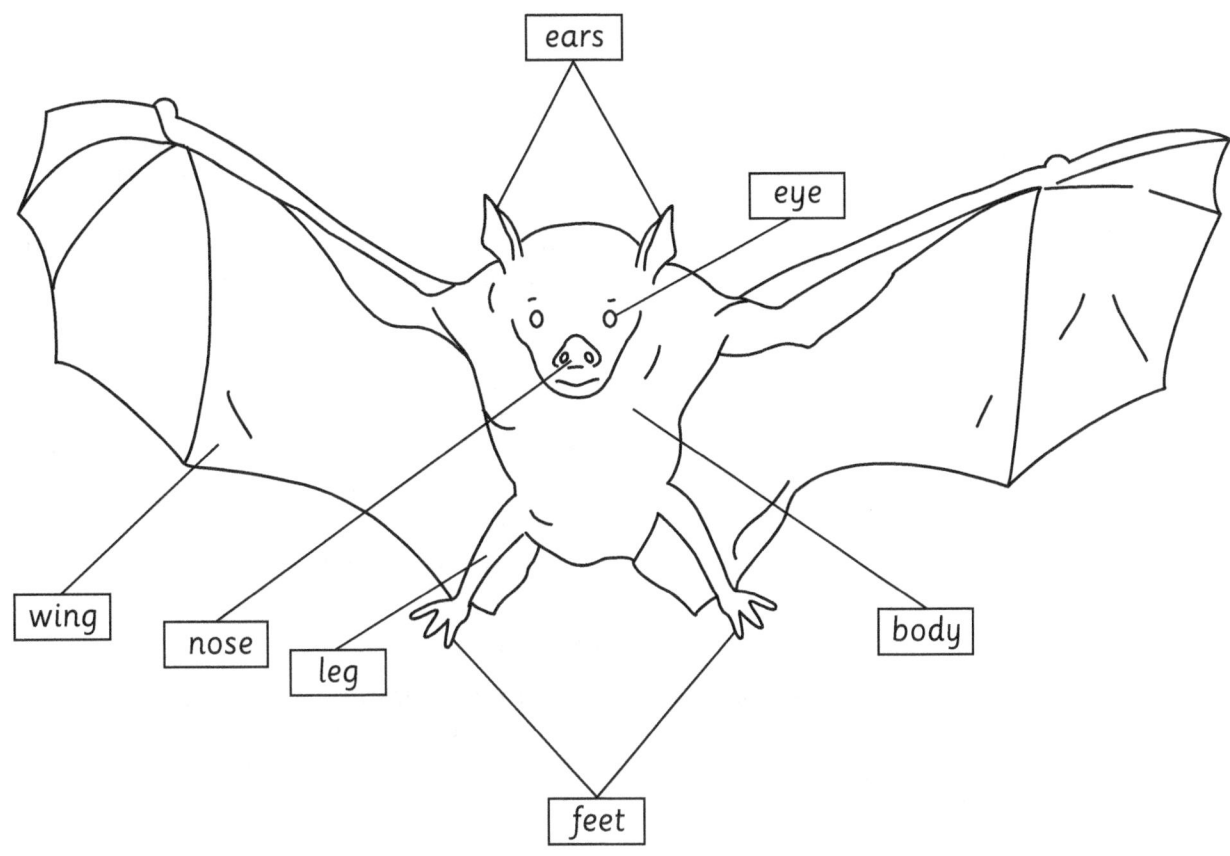

Type of bat	Size	Habitat	Food
fruit bat	wingspan of 1.5 m	trees in tropical forests in Africa, Asia, Europe and Australia	figs, mangoes, guavas, bananas and local fruit
Brandt's bat	wingspan of 25 cm	old buildings, caves and trees in Europe and Asia	moths, spiders and small insects
vampire bat	wingspan of 18 cm	caves, wells and dark places in Central and South America	blood from sleeping cattle and horses

Finding answers in reports

Learning objectives

- Find answers to questions by reading a section of text. (2Rx3)
- Read and respond to question words, e.g. *what, where, when, who, why.* (2Rx1)
- Articulate clearly so that others can hear. (2SL3)

Resources

Photocopiable pages 161 and 163; highlighter pens.

Starter

- Display an enlarged copy of photocopiable page 161 and ask the learners in pairs to get out their answers to the questions from the last lesson.

- Ask each question in turn, quizzing different pairs to tell you the answer and then explain in which column, and in which row, the answer can be found. Keep reminding the learners of the importance of speaking clearly so that others can hear.

Main activities

- Display an enlarged version of photocopiable page 163 and read each report in turn. Ask the learners to tell you which facts they found interesting.

- Give the learners in pairs photocopiable page 163 and a copy of the following questions:
  - How do fruit bats find fruit?
  - Why do fruit bats have very sharp teeth?
  - What is the wingspan of the largest fruit bat?
  - What food do vampire bats eat?
  - What do they use their sharp teeth for?
  - Which animals do they feed on?
  - Where do Brandt's bats hibernate?
  - When do they start hunting?
  - How do they catch their food?

- Tell the learners that when they search for the answers to the questions they should remember that many sentences will have more than one piece of information in them so they have to read these carefully.

- Model locating the information for the first question: finding the section on fruit bats, scanning the passage to find reference to finding food and then highlighting the relevant information 'excellent sense of smell' and 'large eyes'. Demonstrate how to use this information in a nicely worded answer: 'The fruit bats find fruit to eat using their excellent sense of smell and their large eyes'.

- Tell the pairs to work in a similar way to locate information and answer the questions. Remind them to discuss what they are doing and listen to each other's points of view.

- When they have finished, ask selected learners to share their answers.

Plenary

- Organise the learners into four teams and give each team a large piece of paper. Tell them to write down as many facts as they can about bats. The team with the most facts is the winner!

Success criteria

Ask the learners:

- Can you ask a question about bats?
- Why was it important to speak clearly so that the teacher could hear you?
- Can you remember some of the question words beginning the sentences?

Ideas for differentiation

Support: Ask an adult helper to work with these learners, reading and discussing the questions and finding the answers together.

Extension: Ask these learners to find out if there are any bats living in your country.

Bat reports

Fruit bats

Fruit bats have very large eyes, small ears, and small feet. They use their excellent sense of smell and large eyes to find the fruit they eat. They have very sharp teeth to bite through thick-skinned fruit. The biggest fruit bat has a wingspan of 1.5 m.

Vampire bats

Vampire bats feed on blood. They have sharp teeth for making a small cut into the skin of an animal, then they lap up the blood. They feed mostly on mammals and birds. They can walk easily and even run at 2.2 m per second.

Brandt's bats

Brandt's bats hibernate between October and March in caves, tunnels and mines. Brandt's bats come out from where they were sleeping about half an hour before sunset and are active throughout the night. They fly really fast and hunt over water or at low levels and in woodland. They feed on moths, small insects living near water and spiders.

Stacking up information

- Find factual information from different formats, e.g. charts, labelled diagrams. (2Rx4)
- Explore a variety of non-fiction texts on screen. (2R08)
- Explain plans and ideas, extending them in the light of discussion. (2SL2)

Resources

Information books; internet access; photocopiable pages 161, 163 and 165; three envelopes.

Starter

- Show the learners a range of information books (about bats if possible) and ask them to point out some of the features that they see (headings, photographs, captions, subheadings, and so on).
- Focus on the photographs in the book and ask the learners what the photographs add to the page. Ask: *Are they just to make the page look pretty?*
- Agree that the photographs add specific information to the subject – having something described is not as clear as seeing it as a photograph. Talk about how scientists take lots of photographs so they can record exactly what they've seen.
- Display images of fruit bats, Brandt's bats and vampire bats from the internet and discuss what the learners discover about the bats from the photographs.
- Display an enlarged version of photocopiable page 161 and add any extra information that you have collected to the chart (for example colour of fur, and so on).

Main activities

- Ask the learners to work in pairs and give each pair photocopiable pages 161, 163 and 165.
- Tell them to work as text detectives to find out which facts on photocopiable page 165 are about which bat. Tell them to use their knowledge of bats along with the information on photocopiable pages 161 and 163.
- Call them back together again as a class and work through the facts, asking the learners to explain how they worked out which fact matched which bat.

Plenary

- Divide the learners into three groups and give each group a set of all the facts from photocopiable pages 161, 163 and 165 cut up into individual sentences, and an envelope.
- Give each team one of the three bats to investigate and tell them to locate all their bat facts from the pile and put them in their envelope. The winning team is the first to present you with their envelope. (These strips will be used in the next lesson, so keep them safe.)

Success criteria

Ask the learners:

- Are photographs useful for finding more information about something?
- Why are photographs better than a drawing?
- Why is it useful to look at photographs on screen?
- Why is it useful to work together, sharing ideas?

Ideas for differentiation

Support: Assist these learners by pairing them up with good readers.

Extension: Challenge these learners to use information books or the internet to find out if all bats have tongues.

Name: _____

Which bat?

Here are some facts about bats. Decide whether each fact is about fruit bats, Brandt's bats or vampire bats. Write the name of the bat in the table below.

Facts	Name of bat
1. They use sound to catch spiders, moths and small insects.	
2. They can't land very well and often crash into bushes because they have very small feet.	
3. If they can't find blood for two nights, they will die.	
4. They are decreasing in numbers because woodlands are being cut down.	
5. They have very long tongues, which they can roll up and place below their ribs.	
6. They have short noses with big nostrils, which can quickly smell where blood is flowing just under the skin.	

Bat presentation

- Read and respond to question words, e.g. *what, where, when, who, why.* (2Rx1)
- Extend experiences and ideas through role-play. (2SL9)
- Begin to be aware of ways in which speakers vary talk, e.g. the use of more formal vocabulary and tone of voice. (2SL10)

Photocopiable pages 161, 163, 165 and 167; information strips from last lesson; a ball.

Starter

- Ask the learners to return to the groups they were in for the Plenary of the last lesson and get out their envelope of information strips.
- Give each group a set of the following headings on separate pieces of card and tell them to organise their strips against each heading:
  - 'Name of bat'
  - 'Where they are found in the world'
  - 'Habitat'
  - 'What they look like'
  - 'Where they roost'
  - 'What they eat'
  - 'Other interesting facts'.

Main activities

- Tell the learners that they are going to pretend to be a group of scientists who are going to give a presentation on their assigned bat.
- Talk about formal language, and model taking one group's information for one of the headings and combining it to create an interesting statement.
- Tell the groups to discuss how the information is going to be presented. Tell them to nominate a group leader to be in charge of making sure the decisions have been made (not bossing everyone about). Give each group a copy of photocopiable page 167 and ask the leader to fill it in and make sure that everyone knows exactly what they're doing.

- Encourage the learners to find images and other aids such as maps and globes to use in their presentation.
- Ask the learners to practise their presentations a couple of times then run each group's presentation, with you in role as host. Tell the leaders to introduce their presentation.
- After each presentation, encourage the learners watching to ask questions. Have fun making up scientific ways of saying 'I don't know', for example: 'That is an interesting question. I'm afraid I'll have to do more research before I can answer that'.

Plenary

- Sit all the learners in a circle. Ask a question about bats and roll a ball to a learner, who must answer the question. Ask the other learners if they got it correct. Now this learner must think of a question and roll the ball to another learner, and so on.

Ask the learners:

- Can you think of some question words used at the beginning of questions?
- What did you have to prepare for your presentation in role as scientists?
- Why was it important to use a more formal style of speech for your presentation?

Support: Organise the presentation in mixed-ability teams so that these learners take a full and active part.

Extension: Ask these learners to take on the role of leader.

Name: _____

Presentation checklist

Use this checklist to check that you've done everything you
need to for your presentation.

	Notes
Who will be the team leader?	
What role will the other team members have?	
What happens first?	
What happens next?	
And after that?	
Have you practised saying your presentation aloud?	
What pictures or props will you use and are they ready?	

Writing a booklet about bats

Starter

- Tell the learners that they are going to write a little information booklet about these three bats: fruit bats, Brandt's bats and vampire bats.

- Give each learner a blank folded and stapled leaflet and share ideas about a title for their booklet. Tell them to create a cover for their booklet, remembering to write their own name as the author.

- Ask the learners to number their booklet, starting with a 2 on the inside of the cover.

Main activities

- Give each learner three copies of photocopiable page 169 and model how to fill in a page for one bat using the present tense and some sentences that include two facts.

- Tell the learners to create a page for each of the bats they've been studying. Explain that they can colour, cut out, stick on and label the illustrations at the bottom of the page, or use other images from the internet.

- When the learners have checked their writing, tell them to stick their reports into pages 4, 5 and 6.

- Challenge them to create an index on page 7. Ask them to read pages 4, 5 and 6 of their booklet and make a list (on rough paper) of key words, for example blood, vampire bats, fruit bats, feet, and so on, and note every time these words occur. Show them how to organise these alphabetically into a list, then to write the page number alongside to create their index.

- Model how to create a contents page on page 3, showing that they only need to refer to pages 4–7. Tell them to double-check which order their bats are in on pages 4, 5 and 6.

- Finally, they must write a blurb on the back cover, for example: 'Find out more about amazing bats …'

- Explain that they can either leave page 2 blank or add another picture.

Plenary

- Arrange a table-top display of the learners' booklets and ask them to move around in pairs, looking at and reading the booklets. Ask for feedback on which ones they enjoyed most and why.

Making an information page

Use the template below to create an information page for your booklet about bats.

✂ --

_____ bats

Stick your bat picture here

_____ bats live _____

_____

_____

_____

_____ bats eat _____

_____

_____

_____

_____ bats _____

_____

_____

_____

Gathering information

Starter

• Tell the learners that over the next few lessons they are going to find out some information about rainforests. Once they have gathered their information they will use this to write their own report.

• Ask: *Does anyone know anything about rainforests?* Write the heading 'What we already know about rainforests' on a large piece of paper and capture all the facts that the learners already know.

• If possible, show a film clip of a rainforest from the internet, capturing some of the sights and sounds such as misty, rainy forest and some of the animals found there, such as snakes, parrots, owls, lizards, beetles and mice.

• Pass round some information books about rainforests and ask the learners to call out what they see.

Main activities

• Give each learner the top half of photocopiable page 171 (the first two sections) and read through the paragraphs aloud together.

• Run through the meaning of any words that may be unfamiliar to the learners, for example: 'dense' – very thick, 'exotic' – strange, unusual, 'creepers' – plants that grow along the ground or wind up trees.

• Give the learners copies of the following questions and ask them to re-read the report and answer them:

1. Where do rainforests grow?

2. Is a rainforest hot?

3. Are there many giant trees in a rainforest?

4. Are there many types of plants and animals living in rainforests?

5. Whereabouts in the rainforest do animals live?

6. What is it like on the rainforest floor?

• Go through the first question together, showing the learners how to search for the relevant information in the passage of text.

• When everyone has finished, go through the answers together.

Plenary

• Divide the learners into three teams and ask each team in turn to say one fact that they have learnt about rainforests, for example 'Rainforests grow in tropical countries'. The team that can come up with the most facts is the winner.

Rainforest report

What is a rainforest?

A rainforest is a dense, steamy forest that grows in tropical countries where it is hot all the time. Millions of giant trees grow together, draped in exotic plants and trailing creepers. It pours with rain nearly every day and there are no seasons, so the trees stay green all year round. More types of plants and animals live in rainforests than anywhere else.

Which animals live in a rainforest?

Lots of different animals live in rainforests: biting insects, poisonous frogs and snakes, butterflies as big as birds, colourful parrots and large apes.

Animals live at different levels in the trees, depending on where they find their food. Some wander around the gloomy forest floor, while others move through the shady level above, while others spend their whole lives high in the sunny treetops.

Why is a toucan's beak so big?

Toucans have giant curved beaks. They use these to reach for juicy fruit growing on twigs that are too small for them to perch on. Toucans' beaks look heavy, but are really very light. Some people think that the dazzling rainbow colours and patterns on their beaks help them to attract each other.

Toucans like company and live in flocks.

What do macaws eat?

Macaws eat fruit and seeds. They have powerful beaks that can crush tough nuts like a nutcracker. They use their strong claws to turn nuts and seeds around while they are eating. This makes it easier to crack them open.

Some macaws gobble poisonous fruit, then swallow special clay to stop them getting tummy ache!

Angela Wilkes (adapted)

Rainforest birds

Learning objectives

- Read and respond to question words, e.g. *what, where, when, who, why.* (2Rx1)
- Find answers to questions by reading a section of text. (2Rx3)
- Use phonics as the main method of tackling unfamiliar words. (2R02)

Resources

Internet access; photographs of toucans and macaws; photocopiable pages 171 and 173; a nutcracker.

Starter

- Show the learners photographs of a macaw and a toucan from the internet or an information book. Explain that they are going to learn some information about these two birds that live in rainforests, by reading two reports. Ask the learners if they know anything about these birds.
- Display an enlarged version of photocopiable page 171 and read the section 'What do macaws eat?' together, showing the learners how to sound out any unfamiliar words.
- Ask the learners if they know what a nutcracker is and if possible give them a demonstration of how one works.
- Ask the learners some questions orally about the report, for example:
  - *What do macaws eat?*
  - *Why does the report say that their beaks are 'like a nutcracker'?*
  - *How can they turn nuts and seeds around while eating?*
  - *What helps macaws to grip their food?*

Main activities

- Give each learner photocopiable page 173 and ask them to read the report about toucans with a partner, helping each other to sound out any unfamiliar words. Explain any unknown words or phrases, for example: 'to signal to each other' – to make another bird notice them, 'like company' – like being with others, 'flocks' – lots of birds living and flying together.

- Now ask the learners to answer the questions on the page individually. Move round the learners as they work, offering any help as necessary.

Plenary

- Prepare some cloze questions based on both reports and see if the learners can remember the correct missing words, for example:
  - Toucans use their … … beaks to reach for juicy fruit growing on twigs too small for them to perch on.
  - Toucans' beaks look … but are really very light.
  - Toucans like company and live in …

Success criteria

Ask the learners:

- Which question word is used in the heading of the toucan report?
- Which question word is used in the heading of the macaw report?
- Why are questions important?
- When finding answers to questions, which words should you look for in the text?
- How did you work out how to say the word 'swallow'?

Ideas for differentiation

Support: Pair these learners with good readers so that they feel supported and can achieve equally as well.

Extension: Ask these learners to find information on pitcher plants, which trap insects and absorb their juices. Ask them to make a pitcher plant out of clay and show the other learners what happens.

Name: _____

Why is a toucan's beak so big?

Toucans

Toucans have giant curved beaks. They use these to reach for juicy fruit growing on twigs that are too small for them to perch on. Toucans' beaks look heavy, but are really very light. Some people think that the dazzling rainbow colours and patterns on their beaks help them to attract each other.

Toucans like company and live in flocks.

Angela Wilkes (adapted)

Can you answer these questions about toucans?

1. What is the shape of a toucan's beak?

    _____

2. How can it reach for fruit growing on small twigs?

    _____

3. Are the beaks heavy?

    _____

4. How do they attract another toucan?

    _____

5. Do toucans like the company of other toucans?

    _____

6. What is a flock of birds?

    _____

Rainforest poster

- Use a variety of simple organisational devices in non-fiction, e.g. headings, captions. (2Wt4)
- Use simple non-fiction texts as a model for writing. (2W04)
- Begin to re-read own writing aloud to check for sense and accuracy. (2W03)

Photocopiable pages 171 and 175.

Starter

- Look together at the original poster created in the first lesson: 'What we already know about the rainforests'. Now create a new poster on a new piece of paper headed 'What we have learnt about the rainforests'. Ask the learners for as many facts about the rainforest as they can remember.
- Display an enlarged version of photocopiable page 171 and read through the text together with the learners to recap, asking them to point out any facts that they would now like to add to the 'What we have learnt' poster.

Main activities

- Hand out individual copies of photocopiable page 175 (enlarged to A3 if possible) and explain to the learners that they will use this page to create a rainforest poster.
- Explain to the learners that they should write three or four sentences – or bullet points – under each heading, using their own words. Model how to do this by asking different learners to make up a sentence for one of the headings and say it aloud. Remind them to use the present tense as this is used for non-chronological reports. Model orally forming, changing and rehearsing sentences before writing them down. For example:

A rainforest
It is a very hot and steamy place where it rains a lot.
The tall trees stay green all year round.

- Ask the learners to get thinking and writing. Encourage them to say their sentences aloud, orally rehearsing these until they are happy with their choices, before writing them down.
- Ask the learners to keep re-reading their sentences to check that they make sense and are true facts, not made-up ones. Tell them that they can check their facts and spellings with photocopiable page 171.
- When they have finished their writing, suggest that they illustrate their poster with rainforest animals.

Plenary

- Ask the learners to arrange a table-top display of all the posters, and ask them in pairs to move around looking at everyone's efforts and discussing them together. Call everyone together and ask them to talk about any they particularly liked, and to explain why.

Ask the learners:

- Why are labels useful when reading information books?
- Was it useful to say your sentences aloud before writing these on the poster?
- Why did you need to re-read your sentences each time, after you had written them?

Support: Make sure that an adult helper can sit and listen to these learners orally rehearsing their sentences individually before they write them on the photocopiable page.

Extension: Ask these learners to find some amazing information about rainforest creatures and add these to their poster, for example blue-crowned parrots who go to sleep upside-down, like bats!

Name: _____

Rainforest poster

Rainforests

What is a rainforest?

Toucans

Macaws

Rainforest animals

Unit assessment

Questions to ask

- How does a page of information look different from a page in a storybook?
- How can information books be as interesting as storybooks?
- Can you learn new facts about topics by reading information books?

- How can you learn more facts by watching a film and looking closely at real photographs?
- Explain how a chart of information is useful for getting facts.
- What two things have you learnt about writing sentences for information books?

Summative assessment activities

Observe the learners while they play these games. You will quickly be able to identify those who may need additional support.

Glossary order

This game consolidates the learners' knowledge of alphabetical order in glossaries.

You will need:

A collection of words from a glossary of an information book, copied out onto separate strips of paper – a set for each team; paper and glue.

What to do

- Divide the class into four teams and give each team a set of glossary words, a piece of paper and a glue stick.
- On 'Go' they should work as a team to put the glossary words in alphabetical order and stick them down on the piece of paper.
- One team member should then pin their page to the wall.
- Check the lists: the winning team is the quickest one to finish the task correctly.

Say what the word means

This game consolidates the learners' knowledge of the importance of understanding the meaning of words in a glossary.

You will need:

A collection of word cards with the definitions written on the reverse; ensure the learners know the meaning of the words before you start.

What to do

- Work with a small group. Place the word cards definition-side down on the table.
- Tell the learners to pick a card and give a definition for it.
- Ask them to turn over the card to check the definition – if they are correct they keep the card.
- Carry on until all the cards are gone.

Rainforest or farm?

This game assesses the learners' ability to compose sentences with accurate factual information.

You will need:

An animal name card for each learner – half the cards for farm animals and half for rainforest animals.

What to do

- Give every learner a card and ask the class to get themselves into two groups: rainforest and farm animals.
- Ask them to get into pairs and each pair to create a sentence about each of their animals, for example: 'A cow could not live in a rainforest because …' or 'A macaw lives in a rainforest because …'

Written assessment

Hand out photocopiable page 177 and ask the learners to complete the task.

Writing a report

1. What should you include when writing a report? Cut out the headings below and choose the things you need for writing a report. Stick these on a separate piece of paper to create your own 'Writing a report' guide.

✂

Heading

This says what the report is about, for example 'Bats'.

Verses

These can rhyme.

Paragraphs of information

These group lots of facts about the same subject together.

Sentences

These are written in the present tense and have facts joined with connectives.

Description of characters

These help the reader to imagine the characters.

Pictures and labels

These help the reader to understand the subject better.

2. Now use your guide to write your own report on one of the following things:

- One of the bats you learnt about
- A rainforest
- Animals that live in the rainforest
- Toucans
- Macaws

Unit 3C: Poems by significant poets and with language play

Nonsense poems

Learning objectives

- Read poems and comment on words and sounds, rhyme and rhythm. (2Rw3)
- Use the structures of familiar poems and stories in developing own writing. (2W05)
- Demonstrate 'attentive listening' and engage with another speaker. (2SL8)

Resources

Photocopiable page 179; video or sound recorder.

Starter

- Tell the learners that over the next few days they will read and learn poems that are a bit silly!
- Give each learner photocopiable page 179 and read 'On the Ning Nang Nong' by Spike Milligan together with them.
- Ask: *Why do you think this poem is called a nonsense poem?* (Made-up words, very silly content, doesn't really make sense, and so on.) *What makes it funny?* (The sounds of the words, the silly content, and so on.)

Main activities

- Ask: *Is this poem total nonsense? Does it mean anything at all?* Ask the learners to turn to their partner and see if they can make any sense out of it. After they've had time to discuss it, agree that the poem is about three places: Ning Nang Nong, Nong Nang Ning (which is within Ning Nang Nong) and Nong Ning Nang; and agree that the first half of the poem explains what happens in each place and the second half of the poem recaps on the same information.
- Help the learners to learn the poem by heart by dividing it up into clusters of lines that go together and learning each cluster in turn.

- Tell the learners to work in pairs to have fun making up their own nonsense poem inspired by 'On the Ning Nang Nong'. Suggest first that they change the 'N' for another letter to get another silly place – Ping Pang Pong, for example.
- Ask the learners to think of some ridiculous things that might happen in Ping Pang Pong, Pong Ping Pang and Pang Pong Ping. Remind the learners to listen carefully to each other's suggestions.
- Challenge them to put some lines together to make a poem.
- Ask each pair to perform their poem in turn. Film or record their efforts to share with others.

Plenary

- Display an enlarged version of 'Doctor Bell' on photocopiable page 179. Ask the learners to read it aloud, then say what is funny about it.
- Ask: *What do you call a train that sneezes?* (Answer: Achoo-choo train.)

Success criteria

- Does a nonsense poem make sense?
- If it doesn't make sense, how can we enjoy it?
- Do you like the jangling sound of the words in 'On the Ning Nang Nong'?
- Why is 'Doctor Bell' funny?

Ideas for differentiation

Support: Organise for these learners to listen to a recording of 'On the Ning Nang Nong'.

Extension: Ask these learners to discuss and write down which poem they preferred, and why this is.

Nonsense poems

On the Ning Nang Nong

On the Ning Nang Nong

Where the Cows go Bong!

and the monkeys all say BOO!

There's a Nong Nang Ning

Where the trees go Ping!

And the tree tops jibber jabber joo!

On the Nong Ning Nang

All the mice go Clang

And you just can't catch 'em when they do!

So it's Ning Nang Nong

The cows go Bong!

Nong Nang Ning

The trees go Ping!

Nong Ning Nang

The mice go Clang!

What a noisy place to belong

Is the Ning Nang Ning Nang Nong!!

Spike Milligan

Doctor Bell

Doctor Bell fell down the well

And broke his collar bone;

Doctors should attend the sick

And leave the well alone.

Unknown

'More, more, more'

Learning objectives

- Read poems and comment on words and sounds, rhyme and rhythm. (2Rw3)
- Read aloud with increased accuracy, fluency and expression. (2R06)
- Write using a variety of sentence types. (2Wp6)

Resources

Photocopiable page 181; internet access.

Starter

- Introduce the poet Michael Rosen to the learners and watch him performing his poem 'The Michael Rosen Rap' (for example at www.youtube.com/watch?v=RCkM-IJew3Q). Discuss the rhythm and the fast pace with the learners.

- Display an enlarged version of photocopiable page 181 and read 'More, More, More' by Michael Rosen with as much pace and verve as you can manage (it might be an idea to practise a few times beforehand). Read it with a fast rapping pace with just two beats to the line.

- Ask the learners what they thought was funny about the poem. Did they enjoy it being so fast? Read it again and see if they can join in.

Main activities

- Hand out photocopiable page 181 to each learner and ask them to re-read the poem silently to themselves.

- Ask: *Where is the punctuation?* (The poem line-endings provide enough punctuation; it's supposed to represent someone gabbling and not taking time for a breath.)

- *Why does the poem have such a fast pace?* (Because this person can't stop shopping, is late, is greedy.)

- *Why does the poet repeat 'buy, buy, buy', 'me, me, me' and 'more, more, more'?* (Perhaps to make it sound as if the items are calling to the person.)

- *Which are the rhyming words?* (Shopping / stopping, by / buy, shelf / myself, and so on).

- *What happens in the last two lines?* (The person can't wait to pay but starts eating straight away!)

- Model how to write another verse for this poem, for example:
  Give me some beans
  [And plenty of … mmm what rhymes with beans – screams, leans, greens. Yes, greens, that makes sense]
  And plenty of greens!

- Provide the learners with a list of rhyming words such as corn / quorn, peas / cheese / chickpeas, and so on and ask them to create their own new verses, working individually.

Plenary

- Ask each learner to display their finished verse on their table and invite all the learners to move in pairs around the class looking at and reading them, and saying which one they like best.

Success criteria

Ask the learners:

- Can you spot all the rhyming words in the rap 'More, more, more'?
- Why is it enjoyable to listen to someone reading a poem well, with lots of expression?
- Did you enjoy writing sentences that sounded like an instruction, in the first poem?

Ideas for differentiation

Support: Give these learners a ready-made writing frame and a selection of words on cards for them to play around with and then copy into their books.

Extension: Challenge these learners to make a shopping list of 25 items for the shopper to buy and read it out to the class!

More, more, more

Supermarket shopping

I can't stop stopping

I can't walk by

I buy buy buy

everything on the shelf

I want for myself

everything I see

I want for me, me, me

I'm gonna load up a sack

You can't hold me back

I want more, more, more

more, more, more

more's not enough

give me more stuff

crunch, crunch, crunch

munch, munch, munch

Michael Rosen

Tongue-twisters

Learning objectives

- Read poems and comment on words and sounds, rhyme and rhythm. (2Rw3)
- Discuss the meaning of unfamiliar words encountered in reading. (2R10)
- Articulate clearly so that others can hear. (2SL3)

Resources

Photocopiable page 183; pictures of knights.

Starter

- Tell the learners that they are going to learn some tongue-twisters today – short poems that aim to make you get your words all muddled up! Start with a few favourites that have been around for years, making sure that the learners articulate each word clearly as they say them.
- Display an enlarged version of photocopiable page 183 and read 'Peter Piper' together. Start off by reading it very slowly and keep getting faster until you're all in a muddle.
- Teach the learners the following tongue-twisters in the same way:
  She sells sea shells on the sea shore.
  I wish to wish the wish you wish to wish!
  Red lorry, yellow lorry.
- Ask them which initial letter sounds cause problems in these tongue twisters (p, sh, l) and why this would be a useful way to learn these sounds (repetition).

Main activities

- Read the second tongue-twister on photocopiable page 183, 'Night, night, Knight' by Michael Rosen, which is a play on words using words that sound the same but have different meanings.
- Encourage the learners to sound out knight (kn / igh / t) and discuss the silent 'k'. Ask: *Can anyone give me another word with a silent 'k'?* (Knee.) Show some pictures of knights in armour and discuss the different meanings of 'night' and 'knight'.

- Ask the class to read the poem, slowly, then faster, and think about what makes it funny.
- Ask the learners to copy this poem out as part of their handwriting practice of letter patterns and joins, and illustrate it by drawing or cutting out pictures of knights.

Plenary

- Read the final tongue-twister on photocopiable page 182, 'The big black bear', and then display an enlarged copy.
- Ask the learners to practise saying it individually.
- Call the class together and ask individual learners to try saying it without getting any words wrong – or twisted!

Success criteria

Ask the learners:

- Why are tongue-twisters fun to say?
- Which words twisted your tongue in 'The big black bear'?
- Why is it important to say each word clearly and correctly in a tongue-twister?
- Why is 'Night, night, Knight' funny?

Ideas for differentiation

Support: Make sure that these learners are paired up with good readers throughout this lesson so they can experience the sheer fun of these kinds of poems.

Extension: Challenge these learners to create a word-play poem using 'ant', 'aunt', 'allowed' and 'aloud'.

Tongue-twisters

Peter Piper

Peter Piper picked a peck of pickled peppers.

Did Peter Piper pick a peck of pickled peppers?

If Peter Piper picked a peck of pickled peppers,

Where's the peck of pickled peppers Peter Piper picked?

Traditional

Night, night, Knight

"Night, night, Knight,"
    said one Knight

to the other Knight the
    other night.

"Night, night, Knight."

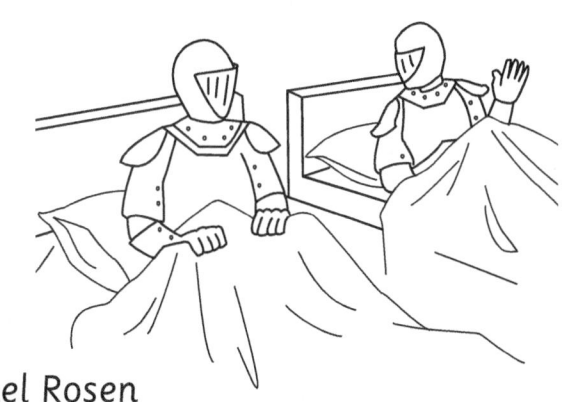

Michael Rosen

A big black bear

A big black bear sat on a big black bug.

The big black bug bit the big black bear,

but the big black bear bit the big black bug back!

Kitty Morrow

More nonsense poems

Learning objectives

- Demonstrate 'attentive listening' and engage with another speaker. (2SL8)
- Find answers to questions by reading a section of text. (2Rx3)
- Write using a variety of sentence types. (2Wp6)

Resources

Photocopiable page 185.

Starter

- Tell the learners that you are going to read a rather strange poem. Display an enlarged copy of photocopiable page 185 and read 'Yesterday' twice, encouraging them to listen carefully.

- Ask them to point out the rhyming words: school / pool, News / shoes, friend / end – which will help them to remember it.

- Ask: *How could anyone go to school the day before yesterday, because it has already happened? That's silly! What nonsense!*

- Encourage the learners to talk in pairs about the poem, asking them to find other impossible things that can't be done. (Going for a walk in a swimming pool, watching a broken TV, starting at the end rather than the beginning, and so on.)

- Ask them what they liked about the poem – was it fun or boring? Ask them to read it several times more and then see how much of it they can remember without the poem on display, using the rhyming words for memory prompts.

Main activities

- Hand out photocopiable page 185 to every learner and ask them to read and enjoy 'One bright September morning' by Michael Rosen in pairs. Ask them to make a list of the nonsense things in the poem, then call them together and as a class make a list of the nonsense elements:

- 'in the middle of July' (it's September)
- 'snow shone in the sky' (snow can't shine)
- 'flowers were singing gaily' (flowers can't sing)
- 'upstairs to the cellar' (cellars are always downstairs)
- 'alone between two more' (it can't be alone if it's in the middle).

- Divide the class in two. Display some sensible sentences and ask each group to work out how to make them into nonsense ones (for example by swapping the verbs over, or changing them, or changing the context):
  - The blackbird sang and the fish swam.
  - I read my book and I painted a picture.

- Call the learners together and check that their sentences *do not* make sense!

Plenary

- Give the learners various starters like these below and ask them to think of some nonsense endings:
  - My laptop was broken so …
  - My purse was empty so …

Success criteria

Ask the learners:

- When you listened carefully to the first poem, what did you notice?
- Can you remember several things that were nonsense and funny in the second poem?
- How did writing 'so' in the middle of your sentence help the meaning?

Ideas for differentiation

Support: Help these learners in the group tasks by asking an adult helper to sit with them and discuss how to make the lines nonsense.

Extension: Challenge these learners to make up their own nonsense sentences.

Nonsense poems

Yesterday

The day before yesterday

I think I'll go to school.

I think I'll take a walk

In the local swimming pool.

The TV's broken

So I think I'll watch the News.

I'll be going out barefoot

In my sister's shoes.

I don't like her,

So I call her my friend.

When I leave

I'll start at the end.

Michael Rosen

One bright September morning

One bright September morning in the middle of July,

The sun lay thick upon the ground, the snow shone in the sky.

The flowers were singing gaily, the birds were full of blooms;

I went upstairs to the cellar to clean a downstairs room.

I saw ten thousand miles away a house just out of sight,

It stood alone between two more and it was black-washed white.

Michael Rosen

'"Quack!" said the Billy-goat'

Learning objectives

- Read poems and comment on words and sounds, rhyme and rhythm. (2Rw3)
- Use the structures of familiar poems and stories in developing own writing. (2W05)
- Articulate clearly so that others can hear. (2SL3)

Resources

Photocopiable page 187; a set of animal name and animal noise cards (see below).

Starter

- Hand out the following animal noises and animal names on cards at random and tell the learners to quickly find the learner with the matching animal or noise: 'duck', 'cat', 'turkey', 'hen', 'owl', 'sheep', 'donkey', 'cock', 'goat', 'dog', 'chick', 'quack', 'miaow', 'hobble-gobble', 'cluck, 'tu-whit tu-whoo', 'baa', 'hee-haw', 'cock-a-doodle-doo', 'bleat', 'bow-wow', 'cheep-cheep'.

- Sing 'Old Macdonald had a farm' and ask the pairs to take turns to say their animal name and tell the rest of the class the noise they make before everyone joins in for the verse.

Main activities

- Display an enlarged copy of photocopiable page 187 and read the poem '"Quack,"' said the Billy-goat' together with the learners.

- Ask: *Why is this a nonsense poem? What is funny about it? What has the poet done?* (Mixed up all the animal noises.)

- Divide the learners into five groups and give each group one of the verses to rehearse reciting by heart. Get them to practise their verse at their tables and then call them together to see if each group can say their verse from memory.

- If possible, record this so that other learners from a different class can listen to it.

- Now challenge individual learners to write a verse where the noises of the animals have changed again, for example:

"Cheep-cheep!" said the billy-goat.
"Quack!" said the hen.
"Oink!" said the little chick
Running in the pen.

Plenary

- Write the following words on separate cards: 'whistling', 'kettle', 'purring', 'kitten', 'ticking', 'clock', 'popping', 'toaster', 'bubbling', 'bathtub', 'gurgling', 'drains', 'roaring', 'lion', 'chirping', 'sparrows'.

- Give the cards to different learners and ask them to come out to the front and stand in the order above, holding their cards clearly.

- Ask the learners holding the sound cards to change places to make some nonsense phrases, as in the poem.

Success criteria

Ask the learners:

- When you first read the poem, did you know what was funny about it?
- Was it easy to write another verse like the ones in the poem?
- Was it easy to understand everyone as they said the poem?

Ideas for differentiation

Support: Give these learners numbered pictures of the animals and matching numbered cards for the noises. Ask them to re-arrange these so that the numbers do not match to create a funny line.

Extension: Challenge these learners to change the whole poem, not just one verse, so that every animal is still mismatched with the wrong noise but this is different from the original poem.

"Quack!" said the Billy-goat

"Quack!" said the billy-goat.

"Oink!" said the hen.

"Miaow?" said the little chick

Running in the pen.

"Hobble-gobble!" said the dog.

"Cluck!" said the sow.

"Tu-whit tu-whoo!" the donkey said.

"Baa!" said the cow.

"Hee-haw!" the turkey cried.

The duck began to moo.

All at once the sheep went,

"Cock-a-doodle-doo!"

The owl coughed and cleared his throat

And he began to bleat

"Bow-wow!" said the cock

Swimming in the leat.

"Cheep-cheep!" said the cat

As she began to fly.

"Farmer's been and laid an egg –

That's the reason why."

Charles Causley

Help

Starter

- Ask the learners if they have ever started off the day in a bad way, for example: got up late, had an argument with Mum or a brother or sister, left their homework at home, and so on. Ask them to share some of their experiences.

Main activities

- Display an enlarged version of photocopiable page 189 and read the poem 'Help' in a desperate voice.
- Ask the learners to tell you all the things that have gone wrong for this person. Ask: *Are these the sorts of things that might happen, even on the worst morning? What sort of poem is this?* Agree that it's a nonsense poem.
- Ask the learners to repeat the poem several times, noticing the rhyming words: right / tight, clock / sock, rose / nose, enough / tough, bread / bed, flies / fries, slug / jug, ghost / toast, mess / yes, No / know.
- Tell the learners that you want them to write some new lines for the poem, then demonstrate how to change a line by replacing the rhyming word in the middle, for example:

There's a clock in my sock

[I could change the word 'clock' for another rhyming word, for example rock, lock, block, croc. Croc is funny – that's short for crocodile.]

There's a croc in my sock

[I could change the word 'rose' for another rhyming word, for example toes, hose – I'll use hose – that's funny.]

There's a hose up my nose.

[That gives me:]

There's a croc in my sock
There's a hose up my nose

- Thinking of rhyming words can be tricky so provide the learners with rhyming dictionaries in print or online (for example at www.rhymes.net/rhyme/).
- Ask the learners to write one new rhyming line or more.

Plenary

- Tell the learners that you want them to bring this poem to life using expression in their voices, and adding gestures to show what is happening.
- Organise them into six groups and ask each group to create a performance of one of the verses. Come together for a class performance.

Help, help

Help, help

nothing's right

I can't find my ears

and my pants are too tight.

There's a clock in my sock

there's a rose up my nose

there's an egg on my leg

and there's a stink in the sink

Help, help

I've had enough

I can't find my eyes

and the going gets tough

There's bread in my bed

There's flies in my fries

There's a slug in the jug

And there's a ghost on my toast.

Help, help

I'm in a mess

Have you got my head?

The cat says yes.

The cat says yes,

the donkey says **No**.

The hamster in the swimming pool

says he doesn't know.

Michael Rosen

Unit assessment

- Are the words 'Ning', 'Nang', 'Nong' real words or nonsense words?

- Why do you think Michael Rosen loves performing and writing so many nonsense rhymes?

- Can you finish this verse?
  The day before yesterday
  I think I'll go to ...
  I think I'll take a walk
  In the local ...

- Why is the verse above so funny?

- Why is the line: '"Quack!" said the billy-goat' so funny?

- Which nonsense poems did you enjoy most of all?

Summative assessment activities

Observe the learners while they play these games. You will quickly be able to identify those who appear to be confident and those who may need additional support.

Nonsense rhymes

This game helps the learners to consolidate their knowledge of how two rhyming words can be put together to create a nonsense phrase.

You will need:

Photocopiable page 191.

What to do

- Display an enlarged version of the table of rhyming words on photocopiable page 191.

- Ask the learners in pairs to select two rhyming words and use them to make a silly rhyming phrase, for example: 'sock in a pot', 'jelly in my wellie'. Ask them to read out their phrase and say why it is funny.

Nonsense sentences

This activity reveals if the learners can understand and talk about nonsense sentences.

You will need:

Photocopiable page 191.

What to do

- Display an enlarged version of the list of nonsense sentences on photocopiable page 191.

- Ask the learners in pairs to choose three of the sentences and to explain to each other why they are funny.

Strange menus

This activity assesses whether the learners can put words together in absurd pairs to make a funny rhyme.

You will need:

No additional resources required.

What to do

- Ask the learners to make up some funny food (for example garlic ice-cream, wellies on toast, roasted teacups, and so on) – the funnier the better.

Give each learner photocopiable page 192 and ask them to read the poem and answer the questions individually.

Playing with language

Baa!

Rhyming words

egg	cot	smelly	sock
pot	bat	coat	hog
mat	log	leg	jelly
wellie	moat	cat	hat
born	trolley	sheep	phone
heap	lawn	pie	goat
soap	bone	ladder	hood
tie	wood	donkey	adder

Nonsense sentences

There's a horse up a tree.
There's an apple in my nose.
"Cluck!" said the fly.
There's a lorry on the mountain top.
There's a parrot reading a book.
"Miaow!" said the octopus.
There's a giraffe on my roof!
"Baa!" said the elephant.

Name: _____

Nonsense poems

There was an old man of Dumbree,

Who taught little owls to drink tea;

For he said, 'To eat mice,

Is not proper or nice'

That amiable man of Dumbree.

Edward Lear

Answer the following questions about the poem.

1. Where did the old man live?

    _____

2. How would you teach owls to drink tea?

    _____

    _____

3. Why did he decide to do this?

    _____

    _____

4. What do you think the word 'amiable' means?

    _____

    _____

5. Explain why you find this poem funny.

    _____

    _____

    _____

Cambridge Primary: Ready to Go Lessons for English Stage 2 © Hodder & Stoughton Ltd 2013